The
New Age
Vernacular

Exposing the worldly language that Christians use.

Andrew Crawley Jr

The New Age Vernacular

website - **AndrewCrawleyJr.com**

Copyright © 2019 by Andrew Crawley Jr

ISBN: 978-1-7339015-0-5

Edited by: Erica James, Master Pieces

Photography by: Still Shots Photography by Ashleigh

Table of Contents

THE QUOTE
CONTACT INFORMATION

SPECIAL THANKS

MY SAVIOR JESUS CHRIST for empowering and guiding me to write this literature for his glory. If there is any letter in this book that's not pleasing to you Heavenly Father, please forgive me. I know that you are able to search my heart to see that my intentions were to please you with every word.

MY FAMILY Ashleigh Crawley(wife) and Olivia Crawley(daughter) for loving and being with me through the process of developing and distributing this project. You are evidence that it is indeed a blessing to have a family.

AUTHOR BRANDON SWEENEY for the information and direction on becoming an author. I couldn't imagine doing this without your help. Thank you for granting me access to your knowledge and experience.

FOREWORD

"Is there witchcraft practiced in the church today? It would seem impossible to think that those who take their time each week to come together corporately to worship the King of Glory might find themselves active in worship and conversation that goes against the Word and Character of God. In Pastor Andrew Crawley's book, we begin to see the insidious and subtle ways the enemy deceives believers, yes even those whom we call "Spirit-filled" Christians, and renders the individual believer and the corporate church powerless and aimless. Pastor Crawley reveals in many examples from the Word of God and personal experiences that just because something looks and sounds TRUE, it does not mean that it is TRUTH. Is it possible that while our preachers are speaking about the final judgment of Satan, that a Jezebel spirit is sitting in the pew of the church planning and operating to destroy the ministry and work of the body of Christ? Dear readers, we are at spiritual war and Pastor Crawley's book warns us, prepares us, and shows us how to root out, tear down, and destroy the works of the enemy in the house of God and in the homes of our believers. Read and reread this book for a whole new arsenal of spiritual weapons that just might save your church, your home and your life."

– **Charles Morris**
Pastor/Founder/President of RSI Ministries
Navarre, FL

"In Pastor Crawley's new book "THE NEW AGE VERNACULAR" he gives a timely word concerning judging. This is one thing that is floating around in many churches "You shouldn't judge". But as he has laid out so plainly for us the Bible teaches that we should judge but to do it in a biblical way. In this book he has encouraged us to exercise righteous judgement to decrease the spots and wrinkles of today in the Body of Christ. This is a good read in a critical hour for the Church."

"This teaching is MASTERFUL AND INSIGHTFUL!!! THE BODY OF CHRIST needs to hear and be taught this. How is it that in the natural we send satellites into the space/darkness to watch our enemies, yet in the spirit we operate in ignorance concerning Satan's plot's and schemes? Then armed services send equipped and skilled people into the enemy's territory to become snipers to kill the enemy... How can we know the plans of our enemy if we're not taught and don't understand the way he thinks and how he may come? Yes, we need this knowledge!!! Thanks so much for this Kingdom Teaching."

"Language is an indication of culture, so much so that culture and language are almost inseparable. Whenever we try to understand a group of people one of the first things we have to do is begin to understand the language they speak. Day Translations, a prominent language and translation study group, actually stated, **"You cannot understand one's culture without accessing its language directly"**. *Fatiha Guessabi, a professor of language and translations in literature,* went even further in saying, **"Language is culture and culture is language"**. It is with this insight and deep understanding that Pastor Andrew Crawley is masterfully approaching the subject of the not so subtle plot of Satan to infiltrate the language of The Kingdom. The New Age Vernacular(language) that is currently being pushed and promulgated by well-meaning and not so well-meaning men and women of influence in this current age is dangerous. Dangerous? Yes dangerous, because as language goes, so goes the culture. If the enemy can get us to adopt his language, he can also get us to adopt his thinking and therefore his behavior. I pray that this book reaches the multitudes and helps to wake up Kingdom Citizens from one end of the Earth to the other. I also pray that as you read this book, Holy Spirit would speak to your heart and that you would allow him to correct your vernacular where needed."

– **Reuel Williams**
Pastor, The City of Faith Christian Center
Millersville, MD

"This book will help believers understand and make them aware of the schemes of the enemy. As people read this book with an open heart and mind they will repent and turn to God. Some will repent as they come to realize that they had been deceived. Others will repent as they come to realize how much they have conformed to this culture. Either way, God will be glorified."

– Brandon Sweeney
Author/Motivational Speaker/Coach
Houston, TX

*"To escape the grips of this world, one must have the **<u>DISCERNMENT</u>** to notice repetitious cycles, the **<u>WILL</u>** to break those cycles and the **<u>FORTITUDE</u>** to continuously go against the grain of what those cycles and the world deems as normal."*

-Andrew Crawley jr

BEFORE YOU START

Every Christian needs to set aside some time to reflect on their life, reasoning and reactions to give an honest answer to the question: Am I God-centered, self-centered or people-centered? Through intricate self-examination, one can honestly determine which of these categories they fall under. With any situation and information that you are presented with, start noticing your mental processing and vein of reasoning. Coupling this with the observation of the way you normally respond, should begin to indicate who you are centered on. Whose feelings do you consider first and the most often? By the way you respond to various situations and information, whose interest do you normally end up defending?

Being God-centered is the only correct way to be. God-centered people are those that look to please God and make him proud. They consider His ways and statutes to the best of their ability. They advocate the ways of Christ and the mindset of the scriptures even at the expense of being rejected and looked at as being "weird" by society. Though they may want to be accepted by man, they are willing to forsake man's acceptance for a God-centered world-view.

Self-centered people look out for their own personal interest. When they are involved with something or someone, the underlying motive is usually, "What's in it for me?" Self-centered people will serve others and may do good works for God, but never to the degree that it interferes with their personal satisfaction. These are the people that constantly and without fail seek instant gratification or the pursuit of it. Self-centered people are willing to get in trouble with others and God for the ultimate pleasure of self.

Please note that being people-centered can ultimately be self-centered. Often times people that are centered on people normally overly consider the feelings of others to the point where their goal becomes to not offend people at any cost. Not offending people serves as a source of self-preservation or the self-perception of it. These are the types of individuals that become more offended by things or truths that may offend people than by the fact that the actions of certain people are offensive to God.

We all must also ask ourselves this question: Do we worship and revere Jesus as a religious symbol or as a person? If we can truly say He is our heavenly father, then consider this thought. If anyone purposely and consistently did things to offend and disrespect your natural father here on earth, how would you feel about them and their actions? We who are saved by His grace should realize that Jesus is no less our father than our earthly father. As a matter of fact, He is more of our father! We need to be mindful not only of the actions of others but also of our personal acts of disrespect as well.

Of course, no one is perfect and everyone does things that may offend God. This is all the more reason to be thankful for His grace and mercy. Though this is true, should we ever be okay with defending, advocating or even making way for things that disrespect and offend our Lord? Of course not. Those that are people-centered and constantly kneel before the Idol of People say with their actions and reasoning that it is okay to offend God if we can avoid offending people. Many times they say and do this without realizing it.

Just as we should trust and have faith in God for everything else, we also need to trust that He knows the best way possible to treat people right. Why is it that many feel and act as though they are smarter than God when it comes to "loving" on the people that He created? At times it may not seem like it but God's ways, statutes, principles, laws and boundaries always offer the best way to treat people even if they may not always put smiles on their faces at the present moment. One thing that is consistent with true love is that it can always be found having the best interest in and a genuine concern for people. Having a genuine concern for others focuses on

3

people being good over feeling good. We should consider the overall well-being of a person over their feelings. It is wise at times to consider feelings, so I am not saying to totally disregard them at all times. I am saying when it comes to administering advice, knowledge, wisdom, rebuke or correction, the people's well-being should be held of higher importance than their feelings. Whenever these two are switched around, it becomes sweet sabotage.

TO SEE THE FOLLOWING INFORMATION CORRECTLY, IT MUST BE READ THROUGH A GOD-CENTERED LENS! In order for this to happen, you must be willing to be open to seeing the word of God objectively while seeking to uphold His interest over the interest of those around you and even your own. The remarkable thing about the goodness and mercy of God is that whenever you choose to uphold God's interest first and foremost, it will ultimately be for your best interest as well as those around you.

INTRODUCTION

Often times we as Christians fail to realize the importance of giving attention to Satan's devices. Indeed, it is uneasy for many to talk about Satan and the kingdom of darkness. This should not be the case as much as it is but when you couple Hollywood's presentation of Satan and his kingdom with the spiritual and scriptural ignorance of the average Christian in this day and age, it gives off the formula that brings us where we are as a whole. To reach for and maintain a level of comfort because of this dilemma, many would say to be careful not to give Satan too much credit. Some like to say, "focus on God and you won't have to focus on the Devil" or "the Devil is not in everything." Some will even ask others: "Why do you always focus on the Devil?"

It is true indeed that Satan is not in everything and that sometimes he is blamed for things that are not necessarily his work. It is also wise to keep a healthy balance because some have gone overboard in satanic obsession. Though all of this is true, the fact still remains that Satan is the adversary. Whenever one has such an adversary, it is wise to be mindful of his strategies and devices. As stated in **2 Corinthians 2:11 (KJV): "Lest Satan should get an advantage of us: for we are not ignorant of his devices."** Here

Paul tells us that because they were aware of his schemes, Satan could not manipulate them. Though the context addressed the matter of forgiveness through Paul seeing if they were committed to his instructions, this verse contains an exceeding principle of being aware of the enemy's strategies so that you will not be taken advantage of by that enemy.

Consider how this principle applies to other areas of life. Take a boxer for example. A great part of preparing for a future fight is studying the opponent. Someone may watch videos of past fights and may even study statistics to become familiar with the opponent's fighting style and areas of comfort. Remember this: knowing of an attack before it happens puts you at an advantage of being more prepared for that attack. Even in the midst of a fight, if you are able to see a punch while it is approaching, it strengthens your chance of being able to defend against or brace yourself for the punch. Even if the punch connects, you are less likely to be stunned by the punch if you see it as it is coming. What about professional team sports such as football or basketball? A part of team practices is to look at game film from previous games not only to better discern their own strengths and weaknesses but also to take note of the strengths and strategies of their opponents.

This important concept brings us to the need of exposing one of the enemy's prevalent, cunning and deceitful modern day strategies

which is THE NEW AGE VERNACULAR. This particular
strategy is important to Satan because he realizes something: A
MAJOR WAY TO PRESERVE THE KINGDOM OF DARKNESS
IS BY CLOSING THE MOUTHS OF THE SAINTS!

What would be the best way to accomplish this? Better than
forcing Christians' mouths closed would be to devise a means by
which they would be willing to muffle their own voice voluntarily.
For this to be done in a way that is not only by choice but also
easily penetrates the world and the church, it would have to become
a merging of language. A great way to smother and muffle the
voice of the righteous would be to seemingly synchronize the
spiritual and natural languages of both the righteous and
unrighteous. If you take a broken "spiritual" language that mixes
partial scriptural facts (not truth) and manipulate it in a way that it
becomes a welcoming pillar for new age ideals, the spiritually
immature and scripturally ignorant would adopt it as "Kingdom
language". This would cause the discerning and scripturally versed
to be at a seemingly "civil war" against the "carnal Christian" and
the scripturally immature who will side with new age philosophy.

THE NEW AGE VERNACULAR has done and is doing just that!
New age philosophy is a major part of the ways of this world that
scripture urges us not to conform to in **Romans 12:2: "And be not**

conformed to this world . . ." A closer look at this text translates "world" into "age".

In Genesis 11, we see the power of a people with a common language unifying around a common ungodly cause. Those who are discerning of the current times are already seeing how Satan is going back to an old scheme of global unity and a universalist framework to set the stage for his end time attack in other major ways. Some of those that are not as discerning will hopefully begin to see this as time goes on. Many saints need to be awakened to the point of realizing that we are and have been in spiritual warfare. As a whole, we also need to remember to keep in mind **Ephesians 6:12 (KJV): "For we wrestle not against flesh and blood, but against principalities, against powers, against the rulers of the darkness of this world, against spiritual wickedness in high places."** Remembering these things will prepare the grounds of your heart and spirit to receive this ministry.

Ah yes, the heart! This piece of ministry will not be seen and received as it should if viewed through the filter of your heart. One of the most widespread issues of the day is trusting in one's own heart. When objectivity is made subject to subjectivity, objectivity becomes extinct in the minds of people.

We are living in a world where there are no more absolutes. There is no more black and white, only gray. People feel that truth is now whatever they want it to be. In reality, truth never changes and will always remain even if many choose not to see it or attempt to twist it. It is vitally important to understand that no matter how one chooses to see or not see truth, it is not truth that experiences hurt, pain, or destruction, but those who reject it because they choose not to acknowledge it for what it is. It is also good to understand that at times the truth may hurt but it is not ultimately harmful for those who agree with it. We see a negative example of this in **2 Thessalonians 2: 9-12 (KJV): "9. Even him, whose coming is after the working of Satan with all power and signs and lying wonders, 10. And with all deceivableness of unrighteousness in them that perish; because they received not the love of the truth, that they might be saved. 11. And for this cause God shall send them strong delusion, that they should believe a lie: 12. That they all might be damned who believed not the truth, but had pleasure in unrighteousness."**

Nothing influences a person to reject obvious truth more than that person's heart. The Bible informs us that the heart is deceitfully wicked. Deceitful wickedness is the most difficult to discern because it is a wickedness that feels righteous! So please beware of your heart not just when reading this information but throughout all of life because the truth does not matter to the one who chooses not to see it. Whenever you are presented with any information, do not ask yourself how you feel about it. Ask yourself "Is it the truth?" Whether through instant discernment or research, the moment you discover the truth about something, accept and become an advocate for it. It is vitally important to understand that whenever someone rejects truth, it can send them on a spiritual and physical detour.

"GOD STILL LOVES ME"

One of the most frequently used phrase of the New Age Vernacular is "God still loves me." The fact that God loves everyone no matter what they do or have done is absolutely true. No one could exist outside of the ultimate grace gift of God's love. Though this is true, many people use it in the wrong way to do the wrong thing. People lacking spiritual conviction or morality concerning a certain topic, action, or behavior often use this phrase to live whatever type of sinful lives and still be considered safe. To better help them cope with whatever they have done or continue to do, as well as to get the Christian or biblical view off their back, they will play the "God still loves me" card.

Please understand, at times we all may need to be reminded that God's love is here to stay and that it is consistent even in our inconsistency. It is knowing this truth that often refreshes a person with the hope, encouragement and strength they need to realize redemption and help with endurance. This notion, though true, can be dangerous depending on the motivation of the one claiming God's love.

Jesus is a person

The "standards of Christianity" would be more healthy, more pleasing to God and laced with more heartfelt effort if the masses truly realized that Jesus is a person and not just some religious symbol. If we related to HIM like the person that HE is, convictions, statutes and commands would make more sense as a whole.

To better understand this truth, think about the relationship between a husband and a wife. It is a horrible thing for an individual to purposely offend their spouse knowing that whatever they do, no matter how much it upsets their spouse, the spouse will not leave them at the end of the day. How does it sound for a husband to say that he cheats on his wife because he knows she will still love him in spite of the adultery? What if a wife says she continues to verbally chop her husband down because she knows that at the end of the day he is not going anywhere? This is totally different from having a heart of contrition because of past failures to the point that you see the love of your spouse as a grace gift that you do not deserve. Knowing that it is undeserved and not promised to be "A-OK" the next time should produce a certain level of value for their love and commitment. This should bring you to the point that you do what you can to not disrespect or dishonor them on purpose because you love them and value the relationship to the point that you simply do not want to see them hurt.

Romans 6:1-2 (KJV) 1. What shall we say then? Shall we continue in sin, that grace may abound? 2. God forbid. How shall we, that are dead to sin, live any longer therein? This is like asking if you should continue cheating on your spouse so that your spouse can continue to forgive you? How absurd would this be?

This is exactly how it should be with the relationship we have with our Heavenly Father. We do not use "God still loves me" to sear our conscience as a coping mechanism that empowers our carnality. Doing this proves that we are out of touch with He who we're claiming we want to make proud. Desiring to please God should translate into striving to please Him in every way.

God the creator, but not the father

What makes this portion of the New Age Vernacular tricky, is that the truth behind the "God still loves me" statement is used to bring factual misdirection. The prime reason why it is not in the best interest for anyone to rest carelessly in the fact that God loves them is for this reason: God loves all who He created but He is not the father of all who He created. **Romans 8:9 & 15 (NLT) states:**

13

"9. But you are not controlled by your sinful nature. You are controlled by the Spirit if you have the Spirit of God living in you. (And remember that those who do not have the Spirit of Christ living in them do not belong to him at all.) 15. So you have not received a spirit that makes you fearful slaves.
Instead, you received God's Spirit when He adopted you as His own children. Now we call Him, 'Abba, Father.'"

We must remember and teach that being born does not mean that you are in right standing with God; being adopted by Him puts you in good standing with Him. In these contemporary times, the masses mistake experiencing God's goodness, mercy and grace for being a part of God's family. To all who do not receive the adoption, as said in scripture, He would say that they are of their father the Devil. **John 8:42-47 (KJV) 42. Jesus said unto them, If God were your Father, ye would love me: for I proceeded forth and came from God; neither came I of myself, but he sent me. 43. Why do ye not understand my speech? even because ye cannot hear my word. 44. Ye are of your father the devil, and the lusts of your father ye will do. He was a murderer from the beginning, and abode not in the truth, because there is no truth in him. When he speaketh a lie, he speaketh of his own: for he is a liar, and the father of it. 45. And because I tell you the truth, ye believe me not. 46. Which of you convinceth** me of sin? And if I say the truth, why do ye not believe me? 47. He that is of God heareth God's words: ye therefore hear them not, because ye are not of God.

Consider **John 3:16 (KJV): "For God so loved the world that HE gave his only begotten Son. That whosoever believeth in Him should not perish, but have everlasting life."** Paying attention to this well-known verse shows that the love of God does not guarantee safety. As we see here, "God so loved the world" indicates that God loves everyone in the world. He loved everyone so much that He offered the world an opportunity to miss out on perishing by obtaining everlasting life through receiving His Son. This verse clearly indicates that though God loves everyone, whoever does not *believe* in His son will perish.

Though we understand that God loves everyone, we must also remember that this includes those that will spend eternity in Hell. The scriptures inform us that many more will end up there than in eternity with Him. The ultimate fact of the matter is that God's love does not guarantee earthly or eternal safety.

"DO NOT JUDGE"

Just take a moment and ask yourself this question. How many times have you heard "you are not supposed to judge", "stop judging", "only God can judge me", or "the Bible says we shouldn't judge" within the past year? If there is any notion that has flooded the Earth today, it is "do not judge." This is one of the most prevalent phrases in the New Age Vernacular. It hits us from every angle- from the pulpit, the pew, social media, Christians and non-Christians alike, Christian leaders, non-Christian leaders, TV and radio. The modern world has become infatuated with the phrase "do not judge" and it makes perfect sense why this is the case. When you have a world that bathes in the belief that you should "do what you want", "be who and what you want", or "believe what you want", it is strategically cunning to embrace "do not judge" as the portal that opens the world to this pandemic of humanism in both religion and secularism.

By adopting this "non-judgmental" vernacular, the church has allowed secularism to infiltrate Christianity. "Do not judge" has influenced many well-meaning, misinformed, immature and carnal Christians to choose to close their own mouths to sin and sinful lifestyles. Over time, closing mouths and ignoring sin mutates into welcoming, embracing and encouraging sin. Sadly,

16

this is exactly what has and is happening and it has caused a rift between those who are supposed to represent Christ. Now of course, this is not a rift that catches God by surprise.

Different types of judgments -

"Do not judge" would not be so bad if the masses used it in the way that was in sync with Biblical teaching but often times this is not the case. One of the biggest mistakes that society makes when it comes to judging is the demonizing of the term, which comes by failing to realize that there are different types of judgments in scripture. There is eternal judgment, earthly judgement, prideful judgment, righteous judgement, judgement only done by God and judgement that God allows and empowers Christians to exercise. There are instances in scripture where "to judge" just simply means "to give proper assessment of".

Judging can be good or bad depending on how it is used. Because society has demonized the term, people (including saints) are now afraid to touch it with a 10-foot pole. This is critical because the negative connotation attached to judging causes some Christians to relinquish their God-given authority to judge. This also causes many to miss out on the privilege of allowing righteous judgment to save them from the damnation that can come from eternal judgement.

It is always important to understand that with everything there is a balance. When it comes to judging, there are those that are prideful and act as if they have never done anything wrong. Even if they say what is right, at times their attitude seems as though they feel that they are perfect when it comes to spiritual and natural conduct. Some seem to forget that it is indeed only by God's grace that they are not in the same predicament of the one they are scourging.

It is good for everyone to keep **Galatians 6:1 (AMP)** in mind when dealing with the wrongdoings of others: **"Brothers, if anyone is caught in any sin, you who are spiritual [that is, you who are responsive to the guidance of the Spirit] are to restore such a person in a spirit of gentleness [not with a sense of superiority or self-righteousness], keeping a watchful eye on yourself, so that you are not tempted as well."** Here is the balance. In this new age, society says don't deal with sin and don't judge. However, the scriptures instead instruct us, (those led by the Holy Spirit) to address it in the right way and with the right attitude.

With this said, let's look at some scriptures concerning "judging". Let's start with the most quoted one given the New Age

Vernacular: **Matthews 7:1-3 (KJV): "1. Judge not, that ye be not judged. 2. For with what judgment ye judge, ye shall be judged: and with what measure ye mete, it shall be measured to you again. 3. And why beholdest thou the mote that is in thy brother's eye, but considerest not the beam that is in thine own eye?"** Most people that quote, misquote, partially quote or, what I like to call, "copy-quote" this passage of scripture normally reference it as if it is ordering us not to judge at all. To stay away from it completely unless one would be in violation of verse 1. A closer look at these verses would reveal that scripture does not say to avoid the action of judging all together. However, they say to be cautious about how and when you judge. In layman's terms, the scripture says don't dish it out if you can't take it.

The Amplified Version furthers this point, so let's take a look at **Matthew 7:1-3 (AMP): "1. Do not judge and criticize and condemn [others unfairly with an attitude of self-righteous superiority as though assuming the office of a judge], so that you will not be judged [unfairly]. 2. For just as you [hypocritically] judge others [when you are sinful and unrepentant], so will you be judged; and in accordance with your standard of measure [used to pass out judgement], judgement will be measured to you. 3. Why do you look at the [insignificant] speck that is in your brother's eye, but do not**

notice and acknowledge the [egregious] log that is in your own eye?" Here the first verse instructs on how to be careful to not judge in a wrong way that would be unfair and to not have a self-righteous and superior attitude as if "assuming the office of a judge". We must be careful here not to add or take away from the text. Based on this text, many would notion that we should not judge because we are not judges. Of course we should be mindful that when judging we should not act out of the mindset that we are the judge because indeed we are not. Though this is the truth, make no mistake about the fact that even though we are not to assume the office of judge, it does not mean that we cannot judge.

For example, **Joel 2:28 (KJV)** reads: **"And it shall come to pass afterward, that I will pour out my spirit upon all flesh; and your sons and your daughters shall prophesy . . ."** This verse is not saying that all of those sons and daughters will become prophets. It is saying that after the Spirit is poured out upon all flesh they will have *the ability* to prophesy. Just because you decide to go out in your backyard one day and play a game of basketball does not make you a basketball player. You were just able to play the game that day. In addition, everyone that cooks food is not considered a chef. It is the same thing here. Just because there was a moment where you prophesied, this does not necessarily mean that you are called to the office of prophet.

Anyone that is a true carrier of the person of the Holy Spirit can be empowered by the Holy Spirit at any moment to prophesy, heal the sick or maybe even interpret a dream. This is also true when it comes to judging. We are not called to the office of judge, but at any moment a carrier of the Holy Spirit is equipped and ordained by God and the scriptures with the ability to judge. Verse 2 cautions us to be careful that we do not judge hypocritically and unfairly because that same measure that we used to judge others will be measured back to us when it comes to us being judged. Keeping this in mind would cause anyone rendering judgment to think twice about considering others when judging them because they themselves would want to be considered.

Again, God's Word is not saying to totally avoid judging. It is saying to be careful and judge fairly so that we ourselves are judged fairly. This explains why anyone attempting to use this portion of scripture to tell Christians that we should not judge would have a difficult time reconciling this notion with **John 7:24 (KJV): "Judge not according to the appearance, but judge righteous judgment."**

Additionally, Matthew 7:3-5 states **3. And why beholdest thou the mote that is in thy brother's eye, but considerest not the beam that is in thine own eye? 4. Or how wilt thou say to thy brother, Let me pull out the mote out of thine eye; and,**

behold, a beam is in thine own eye? 5. Thou hypocrite, first cast out the beam out of thine own eye; and then shalt thou see clearly to cast out the mote out of thy brother's eye. As we look at Matthew 7:3-5, it is important to keep in mind that perfection is not a prerequisite for administering any type of Spirit-led judgment. This plainly states that it is not wise to deal with the small speck in someone else's eye if you have not dealt with the huge log that is in your own eye. When looking at the King James Version of this verse, it replaces "speck & log" with "mote & beam". The Greek word for mote is "*Karphos*" which means "a dry stalk or twig or straw". The Greek word for beam is "*dokos*" which means a beam of wood or beam of timber. Some scholars have argued that given the carpenter's context that both are made of wood. As a result, this verse questions why someone would deal with someone else's sin when he or she partakes in a larger amount of the same thing. Whatever the case, this does not imply that we should become perfect before exercising our God-given right to minister. If this were the case, who could minister being that no one is perfect?

This context is not suggesting to not deal with your brother's mote at all because verse 5 says to first cast out your beam and then you will be able to see clearly how to remove the mote from your brother's eye. In case you have not realized this

22

already, it does not matter what beam you cast out of your own eye, you will still not be perfect, just able to see a bit clearer.

Luke 6:37 (KJV): "Judge not, and ye shall not be judged: condemn not, and ye shall not be condemned: forgive, and ye shall be forgiven." At first glance this verse definitely seems to be a direct and clear command to stay away from judging. It seems to remain that way until we explore this same verse in the Amplified Version. **Luke 6:37 (AMP): "Do not judge [others self-righteously], and you will not be judged; do not condemn [others when you are guilty and unrepentant], and you will not be condemned [for your hypocrisy]; pardon [others when they truly repent and change], and you will be pardoned [when you truly repent and change]."** We are seeing here that this does not mean to not judge at all; it means to not judge in a certain way and that certain way is to not "judge [others self-righteously]." Despite popular opinion, a person does not automatically become self-righteous whenever they judge, bring attention to, or deal with something or someone that is wrong as seen in Matthew 7:1-3.

Dealing with seemingly opposing scriptures

Now, let's just say that there may be some people with reasoning that would suggest to themselves that the Amplified translation is not one that they completely adhere to or may not even like or accept for whatever reason. This would leave us with a verse that seems to mean to not judge at all and other verses that show that there is a place for righteous judgment from other human beings. There are many cases where two conflicting views seem to both have a scripture reference that supports their side of a particular issue. In this case, what do you do? Does this mean that the Bible contradicts itself, giving everyone the freedom to choose whatever side they like the most, or the easiest and most gratifying option? While I will say that there are some issues that may be gray and should not be mountains to die on concerning scripture, they are few and not normally the case most of the time.

There are two things that normally can reconcile opposing sides or seemingly contradicting scriptures together under a God-pleasing Biblical mindset. Unfortunately, as vitally important as these two are, they are the least likely, even by most Christians, to be brought to the table when issues and scriptures are discussed. These two are A SUBJECTED HEART (which enables one to see objectively) and A TOPICAL BIBLE STUDY concerning the matter.

It is important to always start with subjecting your heart to the Holy Spirit. This allows you to see and embrace the objective truth concerning any matter. This will enable you to be married to the truth whether welcomed or not welcomed by others, convenient or inconvenient, or liked or not liked by you. It is important to allow the scriptures to help us realize that the heart is deceitfully wicked. Deceitful wickedness is so powerful because it is a wickedness that feels righteous. We must be careful by understanding that the heart consistently seeks to carry out the power it has to dupe us. Because of this, we must be willing and ready at all times to self-examine our feelings and emotions on any subject, about any person and within any situation. Please remember that the voice of spiritual maturity is one of more intricate self-examination.

A topical Bible study gives a person the chance to come in contact with God's overall view concerning a given subject. Rarely will you find verses that can stand alone without the assistance of context and other verses on the same topic to gain a clear understanding of a specific topic. Taking the time to study various verses on a given subject grants you the opportunity to choose the truth over partial facts. This truly adds biblical understanding to biblical knowledge.

Therefore, when we look back at the scripture reference at hand, you must notice the verses before and after Luke 6:37. Verses 31-38 seem to speak with the fragrance of "do unto others as you would have them to do unto you." Being that this is the case, why wouldn't verse 37 be laced with the same? According to the Amplified Version, it is.

Understand that you are doing unto others as you would have them to do unto you when you judge others in the right way because this grants opportunities for growth and development. If this be the case, then you can begin to understand how rightfully being judged by a fellow Christian can be of great benefit to the one that would truly embrace Godly correction because in their hearts they want to do their best to be like Jesus. Those who truly want to be right should welcome being corrected by others because it gives them the opportunity to straighten the crooked things in their own lives. The degree to which you want to be right with God should be to the same degree that you are willing to receive Godly correction from others.

Any area or subject that you view with an undisciplined heart that is not brought under subjection, and without having done a topical Bible study on it, will be the area that you would not be open to seeing and changing to be more compatible with scripture and therefore more pleasing to God. So it is important to note that if you want the Biblical mindset concerning "judging", look beyond Luke 6:37 alone or any single verse for that matter. Study all the verses that we visit in this chapter, as well as any other verses in the Bible that address the subject, and then you will be more capable of seeing the Biblical view instead of the contemporary, anti-Christian and new age view on the topic.

Let's take a look at another passage of scripture that many fail to address or even familiarize themselves with when speaking of the "judging" subject: **1 Corinthians 2:14-16: "But the natural man receiveth not the things of the Spirit of God: for they are foolishness unto him: neither can he know them, because they are spiritually discerned. But he that is spiritual judgeth all things, yet he himself is judged of no man. For who hath known the mind of the Lord, that he may instruct? but we have the mind of Christ."** This passage not only shows that we as saints can judge but also shows that we have been empowered by something which gives us the ability to "judgeth all things", that being the mind of Christ.

We that are true followers of Christ must constantly remind ourselves that this is a supernatural walk! Verse 11 in this same chapter reads: **"For what man knoweth the things of a man, save**

the spirit of man which is in him? even so the things of God knoweth no man, but the Spirit of God." Romans 8:9 (KJV): "But ye are not in the flesh, but in the Spirit, if so be that the Spirit of God dwell in you. Now if any man have not the Spirit of Christ, he is none of his." Because we possess the Spirit of Christ, we are capable of knowing the things of Christ. Because we have the mind of Christ through the Spirit of Christ, we even possess the ability to see things the way Christ sees things! Because we have the ability to see things the way Christ sees things, we are capable and qualified to judge.

Now I will say that though this is true, we sometimes allow outside forces to cloud our God-given ability. Due to a lack of development and spiritual maturity, saints do not always judge and see things the way Christ would. Sometimes we allow fleshly filters of insecurities due to our upbringing and life experiences as well as personal pet peeves to cloud our Christ-like judgement. At times, it becomes even more difficult to discern while using the filters of traditional church practices and other things that we have become accustomed to and use as lenses of judgment. Such filters can be problematic because they cause many to believe that they offer Biblical judgement when they instead offer manmade judgment by way of the traditions or comforts of man.

Please understand that I would not dare say that true Christians render good and perfect judgement all the time. Though Christians may err in their judgement at times, remember that just because you may misuse, under use, or never use this judging ability, does not mean that God did not equip you to use it in the right way. One must also realize that it is like a smack in God's face when we undermine and reject the qualities and abilities that He has given us.

Many Christians smother their judging ability by way of neglecting, rejecting, or not even being made aware of the fact that they can and should have it. This along with consistent bathing in the discouragement of society to not even touch "judging" motivates the modern-day saint to choose not to make themselves more acquainted with the mind of Christ to identify and address things the same way Christ would. Because of the new age language, instead of acting and living the way Christ would require true believers to, many of them live according to the way the world tells them that Christ would require them to live.

Another passage of scripture that assists in understanding the power and authority that God has granted to the believer is **1 Corinthians 6:1-5 (KJV): "Dare any of you, having a matter against another, go to law before the unjust, and not before the saints? 2. Do ye not know that the saints shall judge the world?**

and if the world shall be judged by you, are ye unworthy to judge the smallest matters? 3. Know ye not that we shall judge angels? how much more things that pertain to this life? 4. If then ye have judgements of things pertaining to this life, set them to judge who are least esteemed in the church. 5. I speak to your shame. Is it so, that there is not a wise man among you? no. not one that shall be able to judge between his brethren?" The context of this passage speaks to being able to settle lawsuits and other civil matters within the church before they have to be taken before courts of law where they will be settled by unsaved people who have no standing within the church. While this is not specifically just talking about judging people and assessing all things, it does show how high the saints are on the "judgement-rendering totem pole".

These verses inform us that the people of God will one day judge the world and even judge angels. Then it goes on to let us know that this God-granted ability and right that will be exercised in the future proves the present-day competence of God's people to judge. Verse 5 indicates what a shame it is or would be if at least one person from the church could not be found to give judgement that would settle a given dispute. Indeed it would be a shame for a people that should be led by the Spirit of God to be found unequipped to deal with matters that arise among them.

A major concept that many fail to realize is the inconsistency of how society defines "judging". If nothing else, this inconsistency should be enough to signal that something is missing with how the world views the judging subject. Why is it that judging is only considered judging when it seems to be something bad, unfavorable or not liked by the recipient? For example, think about every funeral that you have ever attended, seen or heard of. During most funerals, or whenever someone speaks of the deceased person before or after the funeral, people typically mention that they are now in a better place. Family, friends and preachers normally say things that lead to the assumption that the person made it to Heaven. Why is it not until someone would say something about them going to Hell that it is considered "judging"? Judging is judging regardless of whether someone says someone went to Heaven or Hell. If we are going to say "God is the only final judge", then we have to let Him be the judge both ways. To remain consistent about the matter, people should begin to correct others and tell them to "stop judging" when they hear a person say that someone has gone to Heaven or when they make any other favorable judgements toward people.

If you were to be honest, this would seem very awkward and wrong mainly because we have been bathing consistently in the marinade of the ways of this world for quite some time. It is amazing how people can make "good" assessments all the time but are told to stop judging when the negative assessment comes. Sadly, it no longer matters if the assessment is true or not. Remember, A SWEET LIE SHOULD NEVER BE EMBRACED OVER THE BITTER TRUTH. The truth may hurt but it is not ultimately harmful.

What about the statement that "Only God can judge me?" Given the Biblical take on the judgement subject, this statement is not entirely true. According to scripture, others can judge us and we can even judge ourselves. **1 Corinthians 11:31 (KJV): "For if we would judge ourselves, we should not be judged. (AMP) But if we evaluated and judged ourselves honestly [recognizing our shortcomings and correcting our behavior], we would not be judged."** How many people honestly give healthy and adequate attention to judging themselves? It would be in the best interest of us all if we started giving more attention to judging ourselves as opposed to worrying about not being judged by others. God is not the only one that can judge you while here on Earth though He is the only one that can judge you eternally because of your actions on Earth. Normally when someone says "only God can judge me", they are not concerned with how God views them; they are only momentarily concerned with closing the mouth of God's representative that stands before them. Most of the time, the people that use this statement fail to realize that God is all-seeing and all-knowing. They fail to realize that the one that they say can judge them is currently observing them and will judge them.

Why many avoid "judging"

Among the reasons why many people would embrace "no judgement" lies the issue of avoidance. Avoidance offers a detour around conflict. What probably comes to mind now is the person in your family that always says "leave that alone" or "now is not the time to bring that up". This person can normally feel when tension is rising, and to prevent an awkward-feeling moment from arising, they play this card to seemingly keep the peace. It is good to understand that sometimes "keeping the peace" raises the biggest Hell.

The kingdom of darkness thrives off of being ignored and not giving attention to dark areas. Of course there is wisdom in choosing proper times and proper people to deal with certain things within our families but if this has continuously been said over the past couple of years now, one would need to ask "When is the time ever going to be right?" We as a people must realize that all conflict is not bad conflict. There are some instances where the path of healthiness cannot be known unless it is revealed by conflict. The scriptures record cases where conflict is appropriate in certain situations. While I am not saying to run and look for strife and cause fights, I am simply saying let's have balance by having the wisdom to know what battles to face, what battles to initiate, when to face them and how to deal with them.

People embrace the "no judgment" mentality not only because it helps avoid conflict, but also because they have allowed sin to grow and thrive in their own lives. When this is the case, it is easier to ignore the sins of others when unaddressed sin is strongly present and prevalent even in your own life.

Any Christian at a given moment can judge. When just speaking of leadership, there are some that are totally unfit to be Christian leaders and preachers because of their lifestyle or life choices. There are also those that are called but just need to take a break for a while. Everyone has a portion of "unfit" in them because we all battle with the flesh and are not perfect. Take a good honest assessment of yourself and allow God to show you which one of these categories you belong to. Pit stops or delayed starts in ministry are not total failures. They can ultimately set a person up to become more effective in ministry and to not let the word of God be blasphemed because of them. To those who have a warped self-image, battling insecurities and feelings of condemnation about their calling to minister, be encouraged and know this: You do not have to be perfect to preach and advocate a gospel that is!

Again, let me remind you that this is not a commissioning of prideful folks to gather more fuel to destroy or even attack people with the Bible. Yes, we Christians have a Biblical right to judge; however, I am encouraging them do it the right way. They should judge while having a genuine concern for others and without a prideful and self-righteous attitude; keeping Galatians 6:1 in mind. In doing a topical study on "judging" with all the previously stated scriptures, as well as the ones not listed, you will find that the scriptural consensus is the same. Ultimately, the Bible does not tell Christians to avoid judging altogether. However, the Bible informs them to be cautious of when and how they judge. They should fully operate within the authorized rights of judging given and encouraged by God while being sure to not attempt to operate outside of the judging boundaries reserved only for God.

"SIN IS SIN"

Why would you treat and look at your friend differently if they purposely murdered someone because of road rage than if they just flicked their middle finger at someone because of the same road rage? Why is it that you feel that a pastor would need to take a sabbatical from ministry for a while or permanently, if they would be caught in prostitution, drug addiction or found consistently physically abusing his wife? You may even take it a step further and leave his ministry. Why would you not feel so strongly about leaving the ministry if a pastor came out and confessed to overeating on a holiday or jaywalking? The reason is because "sin is sin" is a new age myth that no one really adheres to or truly believe. More importantly, there is not one single verse in the Bible that would support this notion.

"Sin is sin" is another major player within the New Age Vernacular. Church people tend to use this phrase more than those outside of the church. I have witnessed this phrase being used by teachers, preachers, within gospel music, and pretty much everywhere in Christianity. Though this phrase seems to flow from the mouths of church people quite often, the world welcomes this notion with open arms and is glad that it contributes significantly to the new age language as well as new age Christianity.

"Sin is sin" requires the least amount of effort when it comes to closing the Christian's mouth to sin because many actually think this notion is found in scripture somehow. This statement falsely creates the idea that all sin is the same and that there are no sins that are worse than others therefore concluding that there are no degrees of sin. People use this unbiblical statement to send a message that says that no one should have a right to judge because everyone has sin and all sin is equal.

"Sin is sin" has influenced many church folks and Christians to not speak out against the homosexual movement and even go as far as embracing it. This allows many to embrace it on the basis that even if homosexuality is wrong, "I can't speak out on it because I just broke the law yesterday by driving five miles over the speed limit, so I'm no better than they are." This eliminates all human eligibility to reprove and rebuke others because it would require perfection to render it.

Those bound by this type of thinking would have a difficult time fitting 2 Timothy 4:2 into their doctrinal belief. It reads: **2 Timothy 4:2 (KJV): "Preach the word; be instant in season, out of season; reprove, rebuke, exhort with all longsuffering and doctrine." 2 Timothy 4:2 (AMP) preach the word [as an**

official messenger]; be ready when the time is right and even when it is not [keep your sense of urgency, whether the opportunity seems favorable or unfavorable, whether convenient or inconvenient, whether welcome or unwelcome]; correct [those who err in doctrine or behavior], warn [those who sin], exhort and encourage [those who are growing toward spiritual maturity], with inexhaustible patience and [faithful] teaching." If the reasoning behind "sin is sin" is the case, then who could minister? Who could execute 2 Timothy 4:2? There would be no valid human Apostles, Prophets, Evangelists, Pastors and Teachers. This would even actually eliminate the Bible because it was written by people who were not without sin just like everyone else. With this said, the general notion of "sin is sin" cannot be Biblically sound.

The "I'm no better" distraction

Before we continue on any further, I must take a brief moment to discuss the "I'm no better than they are" idea. This is the framework idea that comes out of the "sin is sin" foundation idea. To the degree that this is true or not should not be as important as its made to be at times due to the fact that this distraction has stood in the way of the real issue. Therefore, it is important to understand that it is NOT about being better or attempting to be better, or looking down on others because one may think he is better than the next person. Remember this, it is not about being better; it is about being different. **2 Corinthians 5:17(KJV) "Therefore if any man be in Christ, he is a new creature: old things are passed away; behold, all things are become new."** A human that has The Holy Spirit dwelling inside is a different creature from a human without The Holy Spirit. True Christians must understand that it is not perfection but our differences that make us eligible to warn against sin. As mentioned previously, we are empowered and authorized by God to do what we should do.

When it comes to dealings from person to person within the Body of Christ, a difference of issues, not a difference of spirit, increases our eligibility to deal with one another within the faith. As far as the true church, carrying the same spirit while having differing issues brings everyone to a place of needing to submit one to another because it shows how we need each other. Everyone has some type of issue as well as some type of strength within the body of Christ. If we all walked in a greater level of humility, we would not become big-headed when we serve or assist another brother or sister with their issue. We would still be humble enough to allow others to help us with our issues. This is a major reason why the depression rate is as high as it is among Christian leaders. The vehicle of what church has been made to be, makes ministry a one-way street for leadership. As a result, the average leader continuously pours out ministry without ever being ministered to spiritually, not just financially.

When it comes to understanding that there are sins that are greater than others, how it sounds should not matter. What should matter, however, is if this is true or not according to the Bible. No matter how crazy or non-Christian it sounds, the truth of the matter is that "sin is sin" is absolutely false when it comes to thinking that all sins are equal. Before you totally close this book, thinking that I have lost my mind and I am in error, it is important to understand something. I am not saying that there are such things as good sins or sins that God "likes" more than others. All sins are bad simply because God hates all sin. I am not saying that some sins are good; I am just acknowledging some are worse and carry a heavier weight of spiritual, natural and possibly eternal consequences than others.

To understand this concept better, think about crime. All crime is bad, but there are some crimes that are worse than others. Look at jaywalking vs burglary or speeding vs murder. What about piracy vs terrorism? All of these acts carry a different level of consequence or time in prison. Look at prison time in light of this same concept. All prison time is bad but there are degrees of "bad". Think about solitary confinement. This is an even worse way to experience an already intense punishment. I am not in the business of offering "pride fuel" to prideful people that look down on others just because their sin does not seem as bad as the next person's. In this case, it is good to keep Romans 3:23 in mind:

Romans 3:23 (KJV): For all have sinned, and come short to the glory of God. I do not intend to create a list of sins ranking from best to worst. However, I do intend to share the truth according to the Bible, regardless of how accepted, embraced, or known it may or may not be even within what we call "the church".

Let's take a look at scripture concerning the matter of "sin is sin." We will start by examining some words that came from the mouth of Jesus himself. **John 19:11 (KJV): "Jesus answered, Thou couldest have no power at all against me, except it were given thee from above: therefore he that delivered me unto thee hath the greater sin."** This one verse should be enough to settle the issue. A simple answer to a simple question would be enough to disprove the "sin is sin" belief. That simple question is this: Is it possible that one sin could be greater than another? The simple answer is "yes" and this verse proves just that when Jesus said "he that delivered me unto thee hath the greater sin." It does

41

not require a further translation or deeper research to discover this. To satisfy the possible critics, meizon is the translated Greek word here that simply means "greater". Out of the more than forty times that this word is found in scripture, it uses the same meaning.

Now we will visit another passage that gives an example of this possibility. **Mark 3:28-29 (KJV): "Verily I say unto you, All sins shall be forgiven unto the sons of men, and blasphemies wherewith soever they shall blaspheme: 29. But he that shall blaspheme against the Holy Ghost hath never forgiveness, but is in danger of eternal damnation."** As indicated here, all sins are forgivable except when one blasphemes against the Holy Ghost. Here a greater sin is seen and it being greater is proven in the fact of the weight of its consequence and penalty of being unforgivable.

What about 1 Timothy 5:8? **1 Timothy 5:8 (KJV): "But if any provide not for his own, and specially for those of his own house, he hath denied the faith, and is worse than an infidel."** Here we see that if one commits the sin of not providing for those of his own house, he is worse than an infidel. The key word of point here is "worse". If "sin is sin" was a reality, then this verse would have said "like an infidel" or "just as an infidel". Infidel means unbeliever. This text implies that a person that sins in this way is worse than the state of an unbeliever. These are some strong words. In fact, they are too strong for the "sin is sin" belief.

Take a look at **Mark 9:42 (KJV): "And whosoever shall offend one of these little ones that believe in me, it is better for him that a millstone were hanged about his neck, and he were cast into the sea."** If someone committed this particular sin, then it would be better for him that he be cast into the sea with a millstone tied around his neck. Could the same be said for someone that did not "turn the other cheek" after being slapped in the face? The tone behind Mark 9:42 ultimately attempts to communicate the seriousness of causing a little one to stumble.

Let's take a look at one more passage of scripture. **Mark 12:38-40 (ESV) And in his teaching he said, "Beware of the scribes, who like to walk around in long robes and like greetings in the marketplaces 39. and have the best seats in the synagogues and the places of honor at the feasts, 40. who devour widows' houses and for a pretense make long prayers. They will receive the greater condemnation."** Here we can plainly see that they will receive "the greater condemnation" because of their actions that were listed in the previous verses. There would be no such thing or there would be no reasons for some to receive greater condemnation if there were no degrees of sin.

What about **1 John 5:16 (KJV): "If any man see his brother sin a sin which is not unto death, he shall ask, and he shall give him life for them that sin not unto death. There is a sin unto death: I do not say that he shall pray for it." 1 John 5:16 (AMP): "If anyone sees his brother committing a sin that does not *lead* to death, he will pray *and* ask [on the believer's behalf] and *God* will for him give life to those whose sin is not *leading* to death. There is a sin *that leads* to death; I do not say that one should pray for this [kind of sin].** Here the scriptures are informing that there is a sin unto death and a sin that is not unto death. To show how much worse the sin unto death is, it is recommended that one show not even pray for it.

All in all, if we look at this portion of the New Age Vernacular in light of a topical Bible study on the subject of sin, then we find that this is not a Christian or Biblical notion. It is one constructed out of carnality and lack of awareness. As with other sections, there are other scriptures not listed here that further prove this point when studied closely. Today I encourage you to go, seek and find the Biblical truths waiting for you. In the meantime, let's immediately stop using "sin is sin" because it only leaves room for the perfect to serve in ministry.

"HE WITHOUT SIN CAST THE FIRST STONE"

"Cast the first stone", like many phrases in this new age vernacular, is also used to restrict those advocating true Christian views, morality and convictions. Modern society gets a kick out of the fact that the average Christian has not paid close enough attention to this Biblical story to pick up on when it is used in the wrong way. A strategy frequently used by those who uphold the New Age Vernacular is the coupling of partial facts with partially or misquoted scripture. This tactic preys upon a person's partial ignorance by baiting them with familiar but partially quoted scripture. Consequently, they open themselves up to a faulty belief. Normally, the person not only connects to the familiar but also embraces the misconception that is wrongfully attached to the partially quoted scripture. The Enemy knows that he can deceive people with partial truth. When we hear familiar information, we instinctively accept it as true even if it contains fragmented facts (or what appears to be facts). Normally, as in this case, that which seems to be factual is derived from partially quoted, totally misquoted or non-contextual scriptures. "Cast the first stone" is a perfect example of this strategy.

Let's examine this further. This portion of the language derives from **John 8:7 (KJV): "So when they continued asking him, he lifted up himself, and said unto them, He that is without sin among you, let him first cast a stone at her."** This verse is a piece of the story about the woman that was caught in the act of adultery. John 8:1-11 gives the entire account of this story. **John 8:1-11 (KJV): "Jesus went unto the mount of Olives. 2. And early in the morning he came again into the temple, and all the people came unto him; and he sat down, and taught them. 3. And the scribes and Pharisees brought unto him a woman taken in adultery; and when they had set her in the midst, 4. They say unto him, Master, this woman was taken in adultery, in the very act. 5. Now Moses in the law commanded us, that such should be stoned: but what sayest thou? 6. This they said, tempting him, that they might have to accuse him. But Jesus stooped down, and with his finger wrote on the ground, as though he heard them not. 7. So when they continued asking him, he lifted up himself, and said unto them, He that is without sin among you, let him first cast a stone at her. 8. And again he stooped down, and wrote on the ground. 9. And they which** heard it, being convicted by their own conscience, went out one by one, beginning at the eldest, even unto the last: and Jesus was left alone, and the woman standing in the midst. 10. When Jesus had lifted up himself, and saw none but the woman, he said unto her, Woman, where are those thine accusers? hath no man condemned thee? 11. She said, No man, Lord. And Jesus said unto her, Neither do I condemn thee: go, and sin no more."**

It is important to expose this part of the New Age Vernacular by pointing out its discrepancies in light of scripture. When this phrase is used by Christians and non-Christians alike, the most frequent mistake they make involves equating "casting stones" with the recognizing of sin, the calling out of sin, and the speaking out against sin. This is far from the truth and is totally not what Jesus did within this story. No matter how easy it is to do at times, we must remember that we should not add nor subtract from the text. We get the most out of the scriptures when we simply leave them the way they are.

This will seem foreign to the masses but in paying close attention to this story you will find that Jesus never addressed the fact that these men caught her in sin. Jesus never addressed the fact that the men recognized and called out her sin. They were not necessarily wrong for doing so. If Jesus did have a problem with them calling her out on her sin, then it would be hard to interpret that from this scriptural account. We only have to go on what the Bible gives us concerning this account. It shows that Jesus had the biggest problem with the thing he addressed. Here we see that Jesus did not address the fact that they addressed this woman's wrongdoing. Jesus addressed how they were going to go about handling her wrongdoing that was being addressed. Jesus had a problem with these people having the audacity to kill her because of her sin of adultery. He addressed the stones because they were going to use stones to punish and kill her. So when Jesus said "He that is without sin among you, let him first cast a stone at her", he was saying, "How dare you punish this woman in this way because of her sin when you have sin that is worthy of you being stoned for yourself?" Jesus addressed the casting of the stones because this was the process of seriously harming, if not killing her.

The moral of this story is not to leave sin alone and ignore it. The true moral of this story is do not seek to destroy someone else for their sin when you have sin that you could be destroyed for as well. Be careful how you handle the sins of another because you do not have room to be prideful enough to attempt to destroy someone else because of their sin if you take a good look at your own sin.

In looking at this story, it is evident that it is not about not recognizing, not calling out, or not dealing with sins of others. If this were the case, then Jesus would have been in violation of the same thing that The New Age Vernacular attempts to come against. As stated in **John 8:10-11 10. "When Jesus had lifted up himself, and saw none but the woman, he said unto her, Woman, where are those thine accusers? hath no man condemned thee? 11. She said, No man, Lord. And Jesus said unto her, Neither do I condemn thee: go, and sin no more."** Here we can see that despite the grace and mercy that Jesus extended to this woman that resulted in her being spared from getting stoned, Jesus still ended up dealing with her sin. He told her to "go, and sin no more". He told her to stop doing the things that she was doing that had brought her before him in the first place.

Another observation that further brings out this point is what he said right before this: "And Jesus said unto her, Neither do I condemn thee: go, and sin no more." This proves that condemnation is not simply dealing with sin because right after saying that He does not condemn her; He tells her to stop sinning. These men were planning to damage her beyond repair. Jesus repaired what was damaged and sent her on her way. The main difference that this story was bringing out between Jesus and the men who brought the woman to him was not the fact that the sins of a person was brought up. It was pointing out the fact that the sins that were recognized, were handled in a different way.

As Christians, it is good to ask ourselves - What is the ultimate goal when dealing with the sins, shortcomings, struggles and ignorance in certain areas of others? The goal should never be to embarrass, to compete, to control, or to destroy. This is what those men who brought the woman before Jesus were doing. Never use the shortcomings of others to make yourself appear righteous. The goal is to bring them to their proper place or restore them back to their proper place. This is what was different about how Jesus handled this woman. When dealing with the issues of others, at times we may have to be direct, abrasive, or deal with things that may be embarrassing. If these things are done while being motivated by the proper goal, they should ultimately be healthy and helpful. Remember **Hebrews 12:11 (kjv) Now no chastening for the present seemeth to be joyous, but grievous: nevertheless afterward it yieldeth the peaceable fruit of righteousness unto them which are exercised thereby.**

"JESUS HUNG OUT WITH SINNERS"

Christians and non-Christians alike use this portion of The New Age Vernacular to endorse the freedom of choice when it comes to association, activities and environments. "Jesus hung out with sinners" is a phrase often used to influence Christians to stand down when they attempt to bring conviction to people who choose unwise associations and activities. You normally see this often in Hollywood among musical artists and actors that claim Christianity. In the name of "Jesus hung out with sinners", many believe they have a pass to build unhealthy and unholy camaraderie with whomever they choose to help build or sustain their careers in entertainment. People outside the entertainment field simply use this excuse to defend their ungodly associations with the world. It is here where many claim that it is in the name of using this as a strategy for reaching the lost. The funny thing about this notion is that this strategy does not seem to be a great biblical one for evangelism.

Let's take a look at scripture to see what is and what is not endorsed given this topic. **Mark 2:13-17 (ESV): "He went out again beside the sea, and all the crowd was coming to him, and he was teaching them. 14. And as he passed by, he saw Levi the son of Alphaeus sitting at the tax booth, and he said to him, 'Follow me.' And he rose and followed him. 15. And as he reclined at table in his house, many tax collectors and sinners were reclining with Jesus and his disciples, for there were many who followed him. 16. And the scribes of the Pharisees, when they saw that he was eating with sinners and tax collectors, said to his disciples, 'Why does he eat with tax collectors and sinners?' 17. And when Jesus heard it, he said to them, 'Those who are well have no need of a physician, but those who are sick. I came not to call the righteous, but sinners.'"** The first verse here speaks to a different idea than the one The New Age Vernacular gives off concerning this topic. As seen in verse 13, the people *came to him* and he taught them. What was he teaching them? Nothing more than the message of the Kingdom.

"Jesus hung out with sinners" would not be so bad if those who used it would stop overlooking the fact that while he was with them he was impressing upon them the Kingdom message and the Kingdom way of life. He did not allow them to impress upon Him their carnal mentality of worldly living. What makes "Jesus hung out with sinners" so dangerous is that it is a prime setup for the world to evangelize the church. New Age reasoning embraces the thought that Christians should reach the world by being close friends with the world. This would include partaking in some of the same activities, collaborating with the non-Christians to create spiritual content, and building comraderies with non-Christians as well as anti-Christian organizations. Normally when an artist, celebrity, or average person attempts to claim this notion as a Biblical notion, the kingdom of flesh and darkness normally does the most "reaching".

Verse 14 in the Amplified Version illuminates the picture here even more. **Mark 2:14 (AMP): "As He was passing by, He saw Levi (Matthew) the son of Alphaeus sitting in the tax collector's booth, and He said to him, 'Follow Me [as My disciple, accepting Me as your Master and Teacher and walking the same path of life that I walk].' And he got up and followed Him [becoming His disciple, believing and trusting in Him and following His example]."** As seen here, Jesus did not tell Levi to come hang out with him for the sake of hanging out. He was actually asking Levi to make a life and belief change by becoming a disciple, therefore opening himself up to be trained by Jesus. Verse 15 shows that Jesus did in fact take time to recline and relax while in the company of many different types of people while at Levi's house. This was because he had a group of people following him who had simply decided to recline when and where Jesus did because they had already been following him and listening to his teaching. The scribes happened to notice this happening where Jesus was with a mixed crowd of perhaps believers and nonbelievers and they were moved to ask his disciples "Why does he eat with tax collectors and sinners?" The answer that Jesus gave in verse 17 proved that he had a different type of mindset that most "new agers" lack. As He said in the parallel, Jesus looked at those that were around him as being sick, as having a condition that he could assist in bringing change to. He did not look at them as people that were okay and just needed to not be "judged".

In this instance, some may reference **1 Corinthians 9:19-23 (KJV): "For though I be free from all men, yet have I made myself servant unto all, that I might gain the more. 20. And unto the Jews I became as a Jew, that I might gain the Jews; to them that are under the law, as under the law, that I might gain them that are under the law; 21. To them that are without law, (being not without law to God, but under the law of Christ) that I might gain them that are without law. 22. To the weak became I as weak; I am made all things to all men, that I might by all means save some. 23. And this I do for the gospel's sake,**

that I might be partaker thereof with you." When looking at this text, there are a couple of things that can be pointed out to let one know that the "Jesus hung out with sinners" notion is not what the scriptures advocate. The first and most important one is that Paul carried a mindset that noted that the people lacked the knowledge that he attempted to get to them. This was the gospel of Jesus Christ. In many cases, when people use "Jesus hung out with sinners", they lack this mindset.

Paul's goal wasn't as much to be friends *with* the people as much as he tried to be a friend *to* the people. Paul wanted to create opportunities to minister the gospel to those that were lost; he did not attempt to go to the latest nightclub for the purpose of hanging out and having a great time. Here, Paul was not in it for personal gain; he was in it to expand the Kingdom of God. This is why verse 23 says **"And this I do for the gospel's sake, that I might be partaker thereof with you."**

Usually, people do not use this vernacular for kingdom expansion. They normally look to add to themselves and to avoid rejection from society by partaking with society to have fun while not offending anybody.

Another conclusion that is not paralleled in scripture involves Paul becoming like Jews, those under law, those without law and those who were weak. Paul's goal here was not to become just like these types of people so that they could enjoy one another's company for the sake of friendship. As a matter of fact, the scripture did not list any of these people as having become close friends with the Apostle Paul. Paul used strategy here to become as these people enough for him to be able to break down and penetrate barriers of separation so that he could minister the gospel to them. Paul was becoming "as" they were but not just like they were. This is why we see **"being not without law to God, but under the law of Christ"** in verse 21. This was put here so that the reader would understand that Paul did not become lawless. He just got in their boat enough to give them the gospel. Verse 22 reads, **". . . I am made all things to all men, that I might by all means save some".** This reinforces that fact that Paul's overall agenda was to make converts not friends. Paul nor Jesus was in it to show the world that they had prestigious connections with rich and famous people. They were not in it to be welcoming to sinners and their sinful lifestyles.

Looking at the verses above, we can interpret that the people that Jesus and His disciples were found with were not close friends of Christ with which He remained in constant and consistent fellowship. They were people that Jesus perceived as needing the gospel submitted to them in hopes that they would become spiritually well. The point is not to prove who Jesus' friends were, but that he was strategic about putting himself around the lost to minister to them instead of being friends with them. If anything, this should show that a great deal of Jesus' ministry took place throughout the community and the marketplace.

A great portion of Jesus' ministry was not within the four walls of a temple or a synagogue. Of course He did spend time preaching and teaching in those places as scripture reveals but I would be the first to say that we need to "go ye therefore". Ministry outside of the temples from Jesus consisted of not only reaching out to unbelievers but pouring further into and developing the disciples. Though foreign to most today, it's amazing how Jesus spiritually housed the disciples mainly when they were away from the temples and synagogues. Notice the many instances where they were put into situations for training. How many recorded times were they placed into situations to minister as well as witness Jesus minister, perform miracles and instruct them? It seems that Jesus focused more on them directly in times when they were away from the temple and synagogue.

The church doesn't need to avoid true evangelism by constantly "being in church". Because the church at large finds it's identity by way of a presentation within the four walls on a weekly basis, true evangelism and spiritual development goes neglected. This neglect robs the church of it's communal and regional identity because evangelism are efforts of outreach and spiritual development comes as a result of proper in-reach. Both of these deal with not only reaching out to the community but also with how the gospel and the church is presented before the community.

When in comes to proper in-reach, enough is not being said about the importance of dumping and refueling stations. Everyone needs a place to confess and talk about their thoughts and innermost feelings; a dumping station of sorts. Everyone also needs a place where they are poured into and to bathe in the ways and examples of faith; a refueling station.

For a true believer to get out of these stations what they really need, these stations (not necessarily a physical church building) must have seasoned, trustworthy and like-minded believers. This is why it was good that the disciples were there with Jesus. Not for His sake but for theirs. This is one reason why it was also good that when He called the twelve and sent them out they were sent out two by two.

The "new agers" need to realize that there is indeed a difference between those that we gain strength from by way of fellowship and a sense of community, and those that we minister to *throughout* the community. These two should not be meshed together. This is why we have scriptures in the Bible like **2 Corinthians 6:14-17 (NLT): "Don't team up with those who** are unbelievers. How can righteousness be a partner with wickedness? How can light live with darkness? 15. What harmony can there be between Christ and the devil? How can a believer be a partner with an unbeliever? 16. And what union can there be between God's temple and idols? For we are the temple of the living God. As God said: "I will live in them and walk with them. I will be their God, and they will be my people. 17. Therefore, come out from among unbelievers, and separate yourselves from them, says the Lord. Don't touch their filthy things, and I will welcome you." 1 Corinthians 15:33 (ESV): "Do not be deceived: Bad company ruins good morals."

Again, I would encourage you to pick up your Bible and study. At the end of your study ask yourself, "According to the scriptures, how much harmony did Christ really have with unbelievers?" Those carrying the "Jesus hung out with sinners" notion do not make an appeal for others to choose or present a different lifestyle for sinners to conform to. They normally assist in maintaining a level of comfort in their lives without Christ.

"CHURCH IS FOR EVERYBODY"

This portion of The New Age Vernacular is a very prominent one. Rarely will you come across a person whether Christian or not, or a leader or not, that actually realizes that church is not for everyone. Because this is true, the probability of you believing this is quite high. Now before you close and toss this book, be sure to pay attention to what is and what is not being said. This notion is not only false but also causes more harm than good throughout the Christian belief system and the church at large. There are a couple of things that have caused the masses to adopt and embrace this belief. 1. The attempt to measure up to the world's definition of love. 2. Lacking the concept and understanding of TRUE EVANGELISM. 3. Ambitions to be "successful" in ministry.

1. Measuring up to the world's definition of love

The world has looked and continues to look at the church and say, "You need to be more loving." The church often replies, "You are right." This would seem to be a good thing when you look at the fact that the church definitely could use a major dose of Christ's love toward each other and in demonstration to the world. There is no doubt about it! The church at large is not up to par when it comes to loving in the way that our heavenly father wants us to. What makes this tricky is that the world is not asking the church to have more of the love that God wants us to have. What the world thinks is love is not love but rather a mutated concept that has reduced true love down to just the fleshy acceptance and the embracing of carnality.

The world defines love as acceptance and agreement. This is where the church has gone and is going wrong. The church at large did not check the world's definition of love before it started looking to measure up to it. The world's concept of love does not have chastening, rebuke, correction, uprooting or pruning. The true concept of love includes each of these. The world's concept of love could actually be considered closer to hate instead.

This may sound terribly odd until you seek to understand the destructive and unhealthy ways of enabling. An enabler may seem to be loving and caring until you see the effects of their enabling. I know this very well due to witnessing the effects of the relationship my aunt and great aunt shared. As far back as I can remember, my aunt engaged in a life of drug abuse as well as being in and out of jail. My great aunt would constantly come to her rescue. When my aunt took another trip to jail, guess who would put up money to bail her out? Guess who always paid her bills? My great aunt would rescue my aunt before she ever had any true chances of being held accountable. In addition, freeing her up from the responsibility of paying her bills enabled my aunt to dive deeper and remain in the destructive path that she had known for the majority of her life. Sadly, now that my great aunt is deceased, my aunt, now over sixty years old, still does not seem to be capable of supporting and taking care of herself because she never had to; her great enabler had always "rescued" her from responsibility. Now do not get me wrong; my great aunt was a caring individual who saw all of her efforts toward my aunt as loving ones but she did more harm than good (without even realizing it) because she indirectly funded my aunt's habits.

This is exactly what the world's concept of love advocates for and does. By making the goal to not offend, allowing people the freedom to do and be as they imagine, to enforce agreement, and to undergird mental illness by way of legislation, society is the biggest enabler to destructive lives and patterns of sin. This, just as much if not more than anything else, causes a great divide between many that are claiming the faith. Many Christians and non-Christians actually make the mistake of thinking that the world's concept of love is God's concept of love or should, at the least, trump God's concept of love. This serves as the foremost reason why denominations and other organizations are splitting up over the community of those embracing homosexual activity. Satan has always known this would occur, which is why he has ordered that much attention be given to this attack.

In the name of this form of mutated love, churches are accepting any and everybody, which has caused a growth in tolerance, invitation, embracing, and, sadly, now the celebration of sin. Now I know some would say that just because we invite sinners to church does not mean that we embrace and tolerate their sin and lifestyles. Of course this is true but when you consider the effect it has on the church at large, it is not a good thing. Look at how the church has offered more of a pillar to sin over the past couple of decades. One of the things that aid in this dilemma is inviting everyone to the church. Those that are invited and allowed to remain in the church will have some type of effect on the church and on how others view the church inside and out. This is a major reason why Paul addressed the problem the way he did in 1 Corinthians 5.

1 Corinthians 5:1-2&6 (amp) 1. It is actually reported [everywhere] that there is sexual immorality among you, a kind of immorality that is condemned even among the [unbelieving] Gentiles: that someone [a]has [an intimate relationship with] his

father's wife. 2. And you are proud *and* arrogant! You should have mourned in shame so that the man who has done this [disgraceful] thing would be removed from your fellowship! 6. Your boasting [over the supposed spirituality of your church] is not good [indeed, it is vulgar and inappropriate]. [c]Do you not know that [just] a little leaven ferments the whole batch [of dough, just as a little sin corrupts a person or an entire church]?

The church in Corinth, just like the majority of churches today, was prideful and boastful about their spirituality while having this person remain in their midst. Churches of the modern era are boastful and proud of the fact that those diving in homosexual as well as other alternative lifestyles are welcomed into their churches. Now you may not like this type of talk because you may be asking, "Where is the love for the sinner?" I will address this thought as you read further. You might also be asking "Is there a place for the sinner at what many call church?"

To a certain degree, what Jesus was to the world when he physically walked the Earth is what the church should be to the world now. Understanding this parallel should begin to help bring healthy balance to what is being stated here. Jesus Christ made salvation available to all while understanding that salvation is not for all that it was made available to. Jesus knew that salvation and walking with Him was only for a select few that would be willing to turn away from a familiar way of life and thinking. This is one reason why He sometimes turned and said what seemed to be strange and hard things on purpose to those following Him. He was looking to shave the crowd down to those who really wanted the life He was offering. Christ knew that the crowds included some who were just there as spectators because of what they had seen Him do and what they had heard Him say. Some were there to witness something different just because of the shock factor. Some were there wanting a miracle but not wanting him. Ultimately, Jesus did good things for many but he only took the time to lead and pour into a faithful few.

Take the time to go back and pay closer attention to the times when Jesus withdrew with the disciples away from the crowds. Jesus knew and showed the importance of separating the field from the field house. Think about how important it is to the success of any football team to understand this concept. In order to prepare for what takes place on the football field, they have to embrace the importance of withdrawing to the field house where their fellow classmates, spectators and the opposing teams are not welcomed to sit in with them. This is simply so they can focus on being equipped for the field. The field is the place of execution. The field house is the place of support and preparation for that execution. The church would be more healthy as a body, more effective at spiritual development and better equipped to reach out to sinners if it understood that the field is not within the four walls on Sunday mornings. Most church leaders and attendees will claim to know this already but the evidence that they haven't realized this yet is the fact they continue to strive to bring the world to the church instead of striving to get the church to the world.

Christ understood this perfectly. How many times in the Bible did he invite people to the temples where he preached? Jesus was not on a mission to fill "churches". He was in the business of pouring into some to go and be the church.

There were times when Jesus separated periods of training and preparation for ministry from periods of executing ministry. This did not make him any less loving. It just made him more effective. Jesus was not bound by the world's concept of "love" by way of inclusion. Not only that, but also many perceived Him as being arrogant and blasphemous. Despite it all, He remained Kingdom consistent.

2. Lacking the concept and understanding of TRUE EVANGELISM

For those that would ask "Where is the 'love' and concern for the sinner?", it is in true evangelism. In reading this literature, please understand that I realize the importance of displaying and executing Christ-like love and genuine concern for others. The scriptures let us know that we should do good to all men and especially those of the households of faith. Just because I am telling you that everyone does not belong in the church does not mean that I am casting away the cares for those that need to become born-again believers. I am actually advocating that we love them more by effectively going where they are instead of attempting to get them to come and gather where you are. To understand the concept of true evangelism is to realize that church services held in church buildings are not the evangelistic tools that many believe them to be. If you are going to use church services in a more effective way, then they should come after true evangelism and after true discipleship has begun. In light of scripture, how many times is it recorded where Jesus used the temple as a place of evangelism? Was not the bulk of His discipleship interaction with the twelve disciples outside of the temple? Though this was the case, we would not dare say that Jesus was unloving or had little to

67

no concern for the unbeliever. He just knew what evangelism and discipleship did and did not call for.

Understanding that Sunday morning church is not significant when it comes to effective evangelism would help with a major dilemma that has been plaguing the church for quite some time now. There has been a clashing between those carrying the idea of there being a certain respect level for "the house of God" and those carrying the idea of "letting our hair down" a bit in church to make it more welcoming to unbelievers as well as new believers.

To a certain degree, there is truth in which I agree with both sides. Indeed there needs to be a certain level and sense of reverence while Christian gatherings are been conducted when the believers are offering up worship and sacrifice to God. Now at the same time, I am not advocating for all of the man-made traditions that people think is necessary for worship but does more harm than good. There are many things done in the name of tradition that does more hindering than helping true and authentic worship.

There is also some truth to the "let your hair down" side as well. The church needs to be more understanding of the fact that new converts will not become Apostle Paul overnight. They are babies in the faith and therefore need a certain level of patience and gentleness. Though this is true, I am not advocating becoming more lenient in the church. Sadly, everything is becoming more watered down because everyone wants to be comfortable more than right. This is not the only reason but a major reason why many churches and church people embrace inclusive doctrines and practices during these times. The church invited the world in and now have become too accommodating to the mentality of those that now come. This is one reason why the Bible does not instruct us to bring them in but to go out to where they are.

So where does that leave both of these sides? True evangelism as well as true discipleship helps merge these two views that are actually not opposing views. With proper evangelism and discipleship in place, the unsaved and newly saved persons are granted the necessary Christian interaction to be trained, groomed and matured to the place that by the time they get to "church" they will properly understand the right attitudes of worship and reverence.

Again, this all must come with the understanding that everything does not get done within the four walls of a church building twice a week. I am not saying to totally throw away what many call church services. I am saying that they definitely need to be reexamined to the point where we realize that there is a time and place for everything. Given what we have made church to be, it is not the time nor place where true evangelism and discipleship is to take place.

3. Ambitions to be "successful" in ministry

I would like to start this point by getting you to ask yourself a question. Think about "church" as a whole. How differently would "ministry" be done void of the thirst of prestige and money? If there is anything that has a strong influence on how "church" is run and executed, it is mammon. One of the biggest reasons why there is a push to get any and everybody within the four walls on a Sunday morning is because a church's size and financial status is often the measuring stick of a "successful ministry". As a whole, do you think it is just to make more spiritual family members by which they are engaged and granted access as such? Do you think it is really to add to the regional identity of the church and to expand the true Body of Christ? The answer to these questions is no. One reason why there is much energy given to filling the seats of the church with whoever, is because the more people you can get to come the more people to receive money from, which can invest in the cycle of becoming even more prestigious in ministry. Fortune and fame is the name of the game. Now this is not the driving motivation in every church but it is in many more than most realize. All ministries are not in it to serve mammon. There are a number of leaders and ministries that have pure ambitions toward ministry. Whether intentional or unintentional, most still function in the same system that is designed to track natural success while making spiritual success secondary or of little to no importance.

Large crowds, nice buildings, nice things, full schedules, celebrity associations and the applause of men are all significant when it comes to serving mammon. Now some of these are not necessarily evil, but they become evil the moment they become core motivations. This is definitely a major factor in the "church is for everybody" type of language.

It is important to not get things mixed up here. Again, Jesus made the faith available to all while understanding that this walk of faith is not for all. When the church fails to realize what Jesus realized and why, it will cause problems for those within and outside of the church and the faith. Because the church at large feels that church is for everyone, it causes them to invite any and everyone to the fellowship. Eventually the church will feel a pull to become more accommodating to those that are invited in not only in seating but also consequently in doctrine. Sadly, this is partially the reason why the voice, mindset and doctrine of inclusion is becoming more prevalent throughout the church during this age. Some reading this would say "well that's not our church" and for some that may be true. Of course this is not everyone but there are many that now embrace inclusion and many that have not yet realized that they are currently embracing it. Those that would say "that's not our church" cannot say the same for the church, and many claiming to be the church at large.

"Church is for everyone", along with the voice of inclusion, places the church in a position to invite leaven, enable leaven and empower that same leaven to stay. If we ever forget the seriousness of leaven within the fellowship, it would be good to visit 1 Corinthians 5. Now it is important to note here that the leaven Paul was referring to was a person that was already a part of the church. It is still important to understand that wanting the world to "come to church", without effective discipleship would eventually cause a domino effect enabling the church to become a cocoon for leaven.

Paul was speaking to the church at Corinth about a man that was fornicating with his father's wife. Given this problem, there were a couple of reasons why Paul was adamant about judging him to the point of ex-communication. Paul knew that just as a small amount of leaven could spread throughout the dough, the effects of sin could spread throughout the church. Sin that goes unchecked in the church affects the church in different ways. It not only affects the church internally but also affects the outward presentation of the church. It is vitally important to keep in mind that the church not only consists of seasoned mature believers but also consists of newborns, toddlers and adolescents in the faith as well. It is just as important to keep in mind that those outside of the church consist not only of those that will never receive Christ but also of those that will receive Christ in the future as well as those that may be in present consideration of becoming a Christian.

With this said, unchecked sin within the church could be interpreted as sin that's "not that bad", embraced sin or ultimately not sin at all to those in the church as well as those on the outside. Either way, the church and her message will suffer significantly. This is one reason why Paul went so far as to instruct disciples not to even eat with such a person. It is important to keep in mind that though Paul's instructions seem to be harsh for this situation, Paul was ultimately hoping for the rehabilitation of this particular person. It was because of love and genuine concern for this fornicator that Paul hoped his spirit would be saved in the end. This is significant during this day and age because it assists in proving that you can still punish people, deal with their sins and even kick them out of the fellowship while still loving them and having a genuine concern for their eternal well-being. Sadly, today the world consistently claims that the church is unloving and uncaring. Please understand we are to care and love people in a way that is pleasing to God. However, love that is pleasing to God will not compromise truth or righteousness. It is a love that will stop any interactions that would hinder one's love for God or God's mission and message to the church and world.

It is also important to understand that when referring to the "church", I have been speaking of Christian services and gatherings. Biblically, when we look at such, they were set aside for times of worship, sacrifice, instruction, development, fellowship and safety. I am not saying that there was never a presence of unbelievers in Christian gatherings; however, I am just saying take note of what they were ultimately designed for. Though a couple of instances may be found where someone was evangelized, this doesn't appear to be the case in many instances. Some gatherings were not designed to be evangelistic, they were training and encouraging the converted to be evangelistic. Simply put, there is a time to reach out and then there is a time to teach others to go and reach out. A major problem with the modern church at large is that many times church gatherings are attempting to be both simultaneously. Because of this, neither is being done in the most effective way.

To make better sense of this, think about a fire station. Fire stations, unlike hospitals, are not designed to bring those that need rescuing to the station to be rescued. When is the last time you saw someone bring a fire to the fire station to be put out? Think about it. Out of all of the meetings firefighters have for training, instruction and fellowship, they are normally designed to be shared with other firefighters. Now this is not considered selfish, unloving or uncaring at all. In fact, the firefighters are viewed as being heroes and servants throughout the community because though their gatherings are not really open to people who are not firefighters, their gatherings are geared toward preparing them to go to the fires to rescue anyone that needs and is willing to receive their help!

The church would be more effective if it resembled a spiritual fire station and not a hospital. Now if we couple this with understanding that the true church is not a building but it is the people that sometimes meet in a building, then the next statement would be more plainly understood. I am basically saying let's train and equip the church to go out and take the church to those that need and are willing to be spiritually rescued by the church!

"WORK OUT YOUR OWN SALVATION"

This part of the New Age Vernacular, like most, is one that even if used with good intentions, can be spiritually bad if used outside of its proper context. First off, it is important to understand that this faith will be experienced and expressed through many different ways. Everyone's walk with Jesus will not look the same or be the same. There are many factors that contribute to this fact. Different callings, different purposes, different leaders, different parents, different cultures and different levels of spiritual maturity are just some of the things that contribute to the difference of experience and expression throughout the Body of Christ.

Not only is there a difference within the body but also there should be chapters such as 1 Corinthians 12 that help us understand this truth. This particular chapter speaks of the fact that there are "differences of administrations", "diversities of operations" and "diversities of gifts". We also see chapters in the Bible such as Romans 14 that speak on things like those weak in faith, choice of eating and days, and **"to his own master he standeth or falleth"**. Just as important as it is to know these scriptures and what they are saying, it is just as important to know what they are not saying as well. Both of these chapters not only speak to difference and diversity but also draw everything into oneness in spirit under the headship of Christ.

There are also verses like **John 17:21 (KJV)**, which reads: **"That they all may be one; as thou, Father, art in me, and I in thee, that they also may be one in us: that the world may believe that thou hast sent me."** In addition, **Romans 15:5-6 (KJV): "5. Now the God of patience and consolation grant you to be like-minded one toward another according to Christ Jesus: 6. That ye may with one mind and one mouth glorify God, even the Father of our Lord Jesus Christ."** Take the time to study all of these scriptures to understand the balance of having our liberties within the boundaries of The Kingdom!

The phrase "work out your own salvation" originates in Philippians 2:12. Consequently, many libertines use this verse along with the previously mentioned chapters to create doctrines that support the notion that Christians are at liberty to ultimately tailor their faith to custom fit their likings and feelings. This is dangerously far from the truth. It is important to understand that the differences in spiritual expressions and walks ultimately come from the leading of God and not our tailoring though there is a portion of our actions, choices and thinking that contribute to the diversity. Being guided and directed by God through the person of The Holy Spirit should reflect the type of diversity that will cause the saints to collectively function as His body. Given the element of choice coupled with free will, it is good to realize that even with all of the diversity, anyone under the leading of the Holy Spirit at any given time should never be influenced to act contrary or in a way that is not compatible with the integrity of scriptures or the mindset of Christ.

Let's take a look at the verse on this topic. **Philippians 2:12 (KJV)** states, **"Wherefore, my beloved, as ye have always obeyed, not as in my presence only, but now much more in my absence, work out your own salvation with fear and trembling."** Many of us are likely to quote more of the last part of this verse than reading or quoting it in its entirety. This is not a hard one that requires much more effort to understand outside of noticing what the entire verse says. The first part of this verse paves the way to a better understanding of the latter part. This is simply encouraging authority-pleasing behavior by giving a reminder to maintain the same sense of discipline, character and integrity in the absence of your leader as you would while in the presence of your leader. This further explains why this verse ends with "fear and trembling", which goes unquoted many times when some point to "work out your own salvation." This actually says the opposite of what the New Age Vernacular attempts to use it for. The reason why you work it out with fear and trembling is so that you do it to please the one you fear (God) and not according to your personal likes, feelings and desires.

The Amplified Version furthers this point even more. **Philippians 2:12 (AMP): "So then, my dear ones, just as you have always obeyed [my instructions with enthusiasm], not only in my presence, but now much more in my absence, continue to work out your salvation [that is, cultivate it, bring it to full effect, actively pursue spiritual maturity] with awe-inspired fear and trembling [using serious caution and critical self-evaluation to avoid anything that might offend God or discredit the name of Christ]."** Notice the mindset expressed here that one should have while working out their own salvation. Here it says "using serious caution and critical self-evaluation to avoid anything that might offend God or discredit the name of Christ". This basically spells out not our will but His will be done!

Similar to the chapters mentioned earlier (Romans 14 and 1 Corinthians 12), Philippians 2 also contains the concept of being on one accord and of one mind. This is so important because if we are of one mind, our actions should all align with this mindset. This notion is reiterated throughout scripture to remind us that difference and diversity do not mean freedom to do what you will when it comes to the code of true believers. We must remember that we are not here to ultimately empower ourselves to be ourselves; we are here to give of ourselves for the sake of The Gospel. Any doctrine, train of thought, or belief system that encourages otherwise should be shunned by true believers. Please remember that the moral of this section is this: work out your salvation when you are on your own as if you are not on your own!

"MY WALK IS BETWEEN ME AND GOD"

Normally this is used to challenge people that bring biblical convictions and mentality into a person's situation or circumstance. Simply put, this is an attempt to use spiritual seclusion for the fleshly benefit of carnality. We all would admit that at certain times it is not always easy to hear Biblical answers and convictions when we are faced with certain situations. This is the perfect time for carnality to speak up by saying "my walk is between me and God". Everyone's faith walk is between them and God. Intimate time spent alone with our heavenly father is definitely important. Though your relationship with God is between you and God, it is not between you and God *only*. You should not want it to be because there are other advantages that are added to our spiritual walk because of the fact that this walk is also to include other Christians as well.

James 5:16 (KJV) reads: **"Confess your faults one to another, and pray one for another, that ye may be healed. The effectual fervent prayer of a righteous man availeth much."** The fact that this scripture advises you to share your faults with other Christians supports this point. Now please do not take this to mean tell all your sins to any and every Christian that would listen. This would be very unwise and unhealthy. While I am right here,

81

let me take a small moment of detour for those who may be reading whose attitudes may not be conducive to the confession of others. It is a shame and a hindrance to the body of Christ for you to turn your nose up at others' faults while looking down on them out of a haughty spirit. To be conducive for confession is to be patient, understanding and humble. You must also not be a gossiper! Please remember betrayal through gossip murders trust. When it comes to confession, people need to confide in trustworthy and mature Christians that can obtain strength through intercession. The church at large has been taking a major hit for some time now because of the fact that our pipeline of healing has been clogged. The church will instantly achieve new heights in healing the moment we become a harbor of confession!

Now let's get back to **James 5:16**. Take time to notice the major advantage that is stated at the end of this verse: **"The effectual fervent prayer of a righteous man availeth much."** This is a huge advantage that one would forfeit their own right to have if they do not allow others to be a part of their walk with our Lord Jesus. Not only this but also many forfeit their own safety to a certain degree by not seeking or being open to a great amount of counsel. **Proverbs 11:14 (KJV): "Where no counsel is, the people fall: but in the multitude of counsellors there is safety."**

82

Let's look at another passage of scripture in support of the point at hand. **Ecclesiastes 4:9-11 (KJV) reads: "9. Two are better than one; because they have a good reward for their labour. 10. For if they fall, the one will lift up his fellow: but woe to him that is alone when he falleth; for he hath not another to help him up. 11. Again, if two lie together, then they have heat: but how can one be warm alone?"** I cannot begin to tell you how many consistent tithe-paying church goers that I have come across who felt disconnected. Because they were walking alone, they fell on their own. Over a period of time, falling on their own mutated into falling away. Now of course the church is not the total blame for each and every situation like this one because there is a personal responsibility to be open to allowing someone else into your boat. However, this ultimately speaks to a lasting epidemic that stems from the church equating congregating with community. The body of Christ needs to realize that just because you have people congregating does not mean that they are in communion. Because this has not yet been realized, many continue to suffer and remain spiritually underdeveloped because the church has reduced itself to a congregation for spectating purposes only.

Someone said that the cross was made of two lines. One line is vertical and the other line is horizontal. This symbolizes that we do not only seek Jesus vertically through our one-on-one time where we look up to connect with him. We must also make our relationship with the Father complete horizontally by also seeking what I like to call "the lateral Jesus". When I say the lateral Jesus, I am speaking of the fellow saints throughout the body of Christ that are on this journey just as you are. Yes, yes, yes! I am talking about other human beings that are truly followers of Christ. Our days would be enriched all the more when we come to realize that there are some things that we will not get "directly" from God through our personal connection with Him because He assigned some things to be received only from Him by way of His people. At times some of these things will be provision, direction, spiritual growth, and yes, even conviction and rebuke. It is important for us all to come to realize that THE BODY OF CHRIST MINISTERS. The truth of this matter is that ultimately your walk is between you and God and God's people.

"THE CHURCH IS A HOSPITAL"

Many well-meaning Christians that may not necessarily have any ill will or intent toward the faith or the church use this part of the New Age Vernacular. Though this part of the language may be one of those carrying the least amount of bad intentions or fleshly motivations, it still does not mean that this is void of a negative impact throughout the body of Christ. This phrase can have as negative of an influence on church operations and presentation as any of the others.

"The Church is a hospital" is used as an analogy. Because this is true, we will not look to disprove this statement as if it is plain wrong or in direct opposition of the scriptures exegetically. We will, however, explore another analogy that would seem to cultivate a more effective way of thinking and execution.

In past times where I have either said this, or heard someone else say this, the intended goal involved conveying how the church should function and who you should see in the church. Normally, when you hear this phrase, some people attempt to focus on the types of people that you should not have a problem seeing within the four walls. This would be the spiritually ill. All unsaved people are spiritually ill, so any and every type of sinner should be invited and welcomed in just as a hospital would welcome people with various types of illnesses. Again, this type of thinking is not the most beneficial or effective for the local assembly of true believers. As stated in a previous chapter, church is not for any and everybody. (Revisit the "Church is for everybody" chapter if needed)

Saying that the church should be like a hospital actually hinders Christ's agenda on the earth. One of Christ's main agendas was to make disciples. This is not only one of the major things He came to model but also the instructions that He left for His disciples to do. Disciple-making efforts would take a major blow without the "go ye therefore" element. This is not only what He told the disciples to do but also what He did to reach those same disciples that He ended up sending. Jesus went to where they were and extended the invitation to them. It is important to realize that this was not an invitation to a church service but an invitation to be a part of His life. Many times in scripture, we see where Jesus took salvation, healing, deliverance and information to where the people were. How many times in scripture did we see Jesus tell folks to come to "church" so that He could work on them?

One of the main indications that the church as a whole has adopted the "hospital model" is the altar call. Though there is no scripture for altar calls, they are evidence that the body relies on the "bring patients in and let the doctor work on them" method of ministry. This is not as effective as many would like to think. The average Christian is encouraged to invite unsaved people to church in hopes that the preacher (doctor) will make an appeal that will compel them to receive Christ Jesus. This concept has allowed us to accept and even celebrate the substandard level of growth and development of the general population of believers. Instead of looking to bring people to Jesus, why don't we look toward taking Jesus to people, developing them through true evangelism and discipleship until they get to the place where they add to the gatherings of believers and not just look to take from them? How about inviting people to Jesus before inviting them to "church"?

Of course, before we think about those outside of the church, we need to develop those inside. As Ephesians 4 notions, the 5-fold ministry serves to mature the church to the point where they can do ministry themselves and not forever rely on those leading. **John 16:7 (ESV) reads: "Nevertheless, I tell you the truth: it is to your advantage that I go away, for if I do not go away, the Helper will not come to you. But if I go, I will send him to you."** Jesus looked forward to the day when He would leave the disciples in a physical sense because He looked forward to their maturity. He knew that as long as He was with them they would look to rely on Him, but when He left them, they would rely on that which would be inside of them. Remember this! No matter how good the interactions seem to be between a leader and his disciples, his leadership cannot be proven successful until his pupils are able to function properly without him. The same can be said about parenting. True successful parenting can be determined by seeing the effects of parenting after the child leaves to become their own adult. Jesus would have never been excited at the thought of forever being with the disciples because He was looking forward to their graduation! This is why He was able to call disciples but send apostles.

With this said, we as the church need not be satisfied with transporting people to see "Dr. Pastor". Christian leaders, like Jesus, need to cultivate disciples to send out leaders and ministers who will do the same. **Ephesians 4:12** calls it **"the work of ministry".** This is one reason why **1 Peter 5:3** reads, **"Neither as being lords over God's heritage, but being examples to the flock."** An example leaves a mental impression for future execution. The reason why you set good examples while you are with disciples is so that you can rely on them to execute when you are not around for them to depend on you. The reason why leaders should not lord over their disciples as it pertains to ownership is because it is important to understand that they do not own those that they lead. It is good to realize this so that Godly leaders will not have problems letting go and releasing people when it is time.

This becomes a bit easier to do when instead of being seen as a lost to "their ministry", it is seen as a gain for the Kingdom. There are times when a lost to an individual ministry means a gain to the overall Kingdom. This is close to impossible to see and understand without having a regional identity as the body of Christ. This has led many to say and believe that whenever people transfer from one ministry to the next that it's absolutely not growth for the Kingdom. This is not necessarily true. Though it may not be instant numerical growth, it could be developmental growth that leads to numerical growth in the future if they transfer to a place that matures them further. It is good to keep in mind that elementary school is never in competition with high school.

This is why it is not necessarily good to celebrate lengthy church memberships unless it is those who have a life-long calling to serve in a particular ministry. This is the same reason why it would be ridiculous for students to celebrate being in school all of their life. Students look forward to graduation. Faculty looks forward to retirement and celebrates longevity during retirement. It would be foolish for a student to celebrate longevity because it would show their slowness in development and be an indication as to how many times they have flunked their classes. This could also reveal the lack of good leadership from their mentors and teachers.

If the church should be like anything, it should be more like a fire station instead of a hospital. A hospital is a place where you bring people in to treat them. A fire station is a training place where firefighters are prepared and equipped to go out and rescue people where they are. Biblical ministry as a whole seems to be more similar to a fire station instead of a hospital. Unlike a hospital, a fire station is really only for firefighters and not those in need of their assistance. Is this unloving or showing lack of concern for the surrounding community? Of course not. In fact, the reason why the fire station is only designed for firefighters is so that they can zero in and focus on training and development so that they can better serve the surrounding community. It is in having a heart to serve the community that gives them a mind and heart to train adamantly.

The church can be looked at in this same way. It is a place where Christians come to get trained on how to spiritually serve the surrounding community. Now some may attempt to refute this by way of **Mark 2:17: "When Jesus heard it, he saith unto them, They that are whole have no need of the physician, but they that are sick: I came not to call the righteous, but sinners to repentance."** Notice here that Jesus said He came to call sinners to repentance. Part of the mission of calling sinners to repentance is the training of Christians to assist in calling sinners to repentance.

This is why He commissioned the Christians He pastored into the battlefield in the closing verses of the book of Matthew. Not only this but also in **Mark 2:17** Jesus never made mention where and when He was going to call sinners to repentance. How many times in scripture do we see Christ being alone with just the disciples? On multiple occasions Jesus spent time alone with only the disciples to train and strengthen them for ministry. Please understand that the issue here is only the matter of *when* and *where* ministry takes place for the sinners. We are not discussing the fact that ministry needs to happen to and for sinners. This should already be understood.

One of the biggest reasons why the church has been baited into becoming more liberal, loose with scripture and accommodating to sinners to the point where the church has become the influenced rather than the influencer, is because the church and the world feel that a sign of being loving to sinners is by inviting them to sit in during times of training. Sinners do not have to be at the training to reap the benefits and acts of service that come from the trained. If we viewed the church more like a fire station, we would train and send an army of disciples out in the communities on a consistent basis. Churches would not have to fight over and compete for "members" as much because we would be sending them instead of hoarding them. Please reexamine and reconsider all that we have traditionally thought of church to be so that you would be open to see what it is designed to be.

"NEITHER JEW NOR GREEK"

Some Christians use this part of the New Age Vernacular in an attempt to find scripture to support some specific viewpoints. These viewpoints appear to be proven valid by ignoring and countering parts of scripture that exclude by trying to prove that the "neither Jew nor Greek" notion is inclusive because it eliminates all of the listed distinctions. It is vitally important to remember one thing when it comes to assistance in bringing discipline to our wicked hearts. We should not approach the scriptures looking to find support for what we already feel. Instead, we should search the scriptures to discover what they say about what we feel. If our feelings do not line up with the scriptures, then let's make our feelings yield to what is written. Due to the fact that many do not practice approaching the scriptures with this mindset, it allows for this part of the New Age Vernacular to be used in an attempt to normalize things such as gender dysphoria. Now I know this may seem to be a huge stretch for some that understand, but we are living in times where stretching due to the vain imaginations of humanity is a worldwide fad.

"Neither Jew nor Greek" is used from time to time to attempt to eliminate any prohibitions or distinctions that scripture has concerning gender. The most common way that this has been used is in defense of female pastors within the church. Because "male nor female" is also listed among the distinctions that seem to be eliminated in the verse, many think that leadership positions within the church should and can be open to male or female. Is this indeed something that can be gathered from this text? Let's take a look.

Here is a portion that derives from **Galatians 3:28 (KJV): "There is neither Jew nor Greek, there is neither bond nor free, there is neither male nor female: for ye are all one in Christ Jesus."** To better understand what this verse says or does not say, let's take a look at the surrounding verses. **Galatians 3:26-29 (KJV): "For ye are all the children of God by faith in Christ Jesus. 27. For as many of you as have been baptized into Christ have put on Christ. 28. There is neither Jew nor Greek, there is neither bond nor free, there is neither male nor female: for ye are all one in Christ Jesus. 29. And if ye be Christ's, then are ye Abraham's seed, and heirs according to the promise."**

Considering the surrounding verses as well as the key verse at hand, we can plainly see that this is not speaking of gender dysphoria, gender fluidity or positions that some can or can't hold.

It is important to understand that this passage speaks of nothing more or nothing less than the availability of salvation. Because of what Jesus did, salvation is accessible to all regardless if any are Jew, Greek, bond, free, male or female. The New Age Vernacular fails in its unbiblical notion of this idea by failing to realize that this idea includes all of these things and does not exclude any of these things. God did not eliminate Jews or Greeks or males or females. Yes, in Him we are a new creation, but He did not come up with some different type of species to where there are no longer any of these listed things. Because of His grace and mercy, anyone can become a part of the body of Christ whether being Jew, Greek, bond, free, male or female. Regardless of what some attempt to make this verse out to be, this is not speaking of who can or cannot hold a position of authority within the church and does not give people the freedom to choose or eliminate their gender. This phrase simply says that no matter the race, condition or gender, anyone can receive salvation through Jesus and be joined to the body of Christ. Any attempt to make this say anything else would be adding something to the text that's simply not there.

"LOVE = ACCEPTANCE"

This portion of The New Age Vernacular is unique and not unique at the same time. Just as all the others, it is ultimately pointing to a new age mindset that is anti-Christ. However, "love = acceptance" is one idea that many times goes without being spoken because in many cases it is expected and assumed to be understood. If there is one thing that gets in the way of spreading true Christian love, it is the mutation of the true definition of love. Society has significantly changed the meaning of love by declaring it as something else. That something else is acceptance. Many times, when someone says "you need to be more loving" they are actually saying that you need to be more accepting. In those instances, you can look that person right in the face and reply by saying "I am currently being loving".

If we are going to continue steadfastly in doing the work of Christ, as Christ would have us to do it, then we must understand a simple truth: acceptance can sometimes be found in love but acceptance itself does not equate to love. As a matter of fact, non-acceptance can sometimes be found in love as well. We must first make the distinction between accepting a person and accepting the actions or lifestyles of a person. Because of this truth, it is wrong when anyone attempts to equate love with acceptance. Often times, this is done in an attempt to lower a standard. As a result, there will be more ignoring or allowing of a particular sinful act or lifestyle, while empowering the mentalities that are compatible with it. The "love = acceptance" portion of the New Age Vernacular is a seed that ultimately yields poisonous fruit. Once the seed of acceptance is planted, it gives way to allowance. Allowance opens the door to it being permitted. Please understand that allowance differs from something being permitted. To allow for something is to give way to or to allocate for something without rebuttal. To permit something is to actually grant authorization. The permitting of a thing paves the way to the embracing of that thing. Once embraced, it can be endorsed. Endorsement gives reason for protection and ultimately the enforcement of that thing.

Mainstream Christianity often fail to realize that our refusal to accept others' sinful lifestyles is often the catalyst for self-examination. This can ultimately lead to a personal conviction, causing the individual to acknowledge that their actions are unacceptable to God, and therefore should be unacceptable to them as well. It seems as though we as the church have forgotten that many look to us for the moral standard in society. Even if they do not even like us or accept our Jesus, they will never say it and in many cases may not even realize it. To this very day, many non-believers feel inwardly that if Christians embrace something then that thing is purified to a certain degree. Now of course this continues to fade as the hours pass but it still and will always be important that the world, as well as those within the church never see the saints embracing and endorsing sinful acts and lifestyles.

This is a major reason why the Apostle Paul instructed the church to not keep company or even as much as eat with certain types of people that claimed to be Christians in 1 Corinthians 5.

True love will sometimes reject certain choices and lifestyles of those closest to you because love has to be unaccepting of some things if it is going to truly have the best interest of a person or persons in mind. This is clearly seen when we look at the relationship between parents and their children. This is the reason why many parents do not accept bad grades from their children, why they do not accept their children wanting to play in or near the street. It is simply because the love that they have for them also comes automatically equipped with a genuine concern for their safety and well-being. This should be the similar type of love that Christians should give to Christian and non-Christian adults as well. Not just for their natural well-being, but we should be just as concerned if not more concerned for their spiritual well-being.

This should allow us to reject anything that is or would be

spiritually hazardous to anyone in the future. This is why **Hebrews 12:6 (NLT)** says, **"For the LORD disciplines those he loves, and he punishes each one he accepts as his child."** The Lord is not out to be mean. He intends to keep us within healthy boundaries and to steer us into ways that are best for us now and for us in the future.

We as true followers of Christ must understand that regardless of how it feels and seems at times we do people a disservice when we are accepting of certain behaviors, actions and lifestyles. It is like we are patting them on the back for sipping poison. Remember to always be wise in your rejecting of things and certain people. There are times where there is no way around being straight forward. Whatever the case, be sure that whenever the time calls for it, be intentional about what you accept and do not accept. This is exactly why Satan is so very strategic in attempting to get the Christian's mouth to close. He knows that the very disapproval coming from a true Christian is powerful enough to plant a seed that can initiate the self-examination that leads to conviction and ultimately repentance.

"CONVICTION = CONDEMNATION"

There are times when we as people misunderstand, misrepresent and misinterpret things. Whether knowingly or unknowingly, we just simply get things wrong sometimes. There are times when many get things wrong, whether spiritual or non-spiritual, because of the fact that we join two words or concepts together to mean the same thing when they in fact are two completely different things. The New Age Vernacular definitely capitalizes on this idea by making this dangerous concept a part of its strategy when it merges conviction and condemnation to seduce the contemporary masses into looking at them both as if they are the same. This is a major advantage for new age strategy because treating these two as if they are the same sets the stage for one of their ultimate goals- the elimination of conviction.

Many would never just throw away conviction if it were correctly defined and understood. It is not until you take something as pure as conviction and marry it to something as negative as condemnation that would lead one to see it as a good thing to discard conviction.

We all know that condemnation is bad for someone to do to another individual. This sort of thing should not be touched. When you get society to see conviction as if it is condemnation by blurring the lines that make a distinction between the two, society would then not want to touch conviction. It is at this point that the world will just overcorrect by demonizing both to make sure that they do not violate the one.

Let's continue by "unblurring" the line of distinction between these two words. In Greek, the word condemnation is translated to "katakrima". Katakrima means *"damnatory sentence"*. Its meaning relates to the rendering of punishment that comes as a result of the determination of guilt. Now when we go back and look at the widely quoted but misunderstood scripture of Romans 8:1, we can get a clearer picture of what Paul was saying. **Romans 8:1 (KJV) "There is therefore now no condemnation to them which are in Christ Jesus, who walk not after the flesh, but after the Spirit."** He was not saying that now there is no more feeling guilty or convicted for those who are in Christ. As a matter of fact, this is not about a feeling at all; it is about the act of sentencing or executing as an act of punishment. He was saying that those who are in Christ will not have a damnable sentencing because of Christ and His ultimate sacrifice. This verse should never be used to be excused from Christians saying what the Bible

101

says about a certain person or action. This verse should remind us all the more of the grace of God that allows those that are truly in Christ to escape a well-deserved damnable sentencing that all who are outside of Christ will experience. Though this should give any Christian a sense of security and feeling of how God sees worth in us, the term at hand does not technically define a particular feeling.

Let's revisit another instance in the Bible. **John 8:10-11 (KJV)** reads: **"When Jesus had lifted up himself, and saw none but the woman, he said unto her, Woman, where are those thine accusers? hath no man condemned thee? She said, No man, Lord. And Jesus said unto her, Neither do I condemn thee: go, and sin no more."** The word "condemn" here is the Greek word "katakrino" which is similar to and short for what was mentioned earlier. As we discussed in a previous chapter, Jesus did not necessarily have a problem with the men recognizing this woman's wrongdoing as much as He had a problem with them condemning her to the point of sentencing her to death because of her deeds. Even though Jesus was the only one there who did not have sin, He looked at her and told her that He was not going to sentence her to death either. At that moment, Jesus gave her what the state of North Carolina justice system knows as a "Prayer For Judgment" and sentenced her to another chance. This is why He told her "go and sin no more." Again, it is important to realize that this is not speaking of how someone feels after something is said to them. This is not a feeling but an act of how something is handled after an assessment.

Before proceeding any further, it is necessary to highlight that the way a person feels should not be the end all be all to how condemnation or conviction is defined. As a matter of fact, a person can feel just as bad with either one in the picture. Condemnation can set people up for doom as it has no place for correction and redemption. Conviction sets people up to correction to the point that they can start or continue walking as the redeemed. Conviction is what creates the need and motivation for correction. Through the years, I have taught the following phrase: CONVICTION opens the door to CORRECTION and CORRECTION gives birth to GROWTH. Condemnation does not allow for any of these things to occur. As stated earlier, this is the reason why Jesus had a problem with the people that had brought the woman to him. It was not that they were wrong in calling out her sin of adultery and recognizing it; they were wrong in the eyes of Jesus because they intended to deal with her wrongdoings in such a way that she had no grace room or chance to correct and be redeemed from her wrongdoings. This is exactly what Christ granted her after the accusers had left.

Let's take a look at the term "conviction". Convict or "elegcho" means "to show one his fault". Merriam-Webster defines "conviction" as the act of convincing a person of error or of compelling the admission of a truth. One thing that we seem to miss in the understanding of conviction is that it is up to the person receiving it to choose how they are going to feel as a result of conviction. At times a person can influence the feelings of the one receiving conviction based on how things are presented. Though this is true, just because someone feels shameful as a result of conviction does not necessarily mean that the person assisting in bringing the conviction actually placed shame on the individual. The receiver ultimately chooses how they receive conviction as well as what they are going to do with that same conviction.

This is what we must understand about conviction. In essence, it is not based on what a person says or does to another individual. As a matter of fact, conviction cannot exist unless there is evil, error or immaturity already found dwelling within a person. When a person comes, they simply bring light to shine on a dark place, a place of error, or an underdeveloped place. As a result, conviction can arise much similar to steam emerging from water being thrown on something hot. It is not that you brought the steam; you brought the thing that caused the steam to happen.

Notice how I stated that conviction "CAN" come out. This is because even with the perfect combination that could bring conviction it may not always happen because a key element to proper conviction is how the one who should be convicted sees their darkness, error or immaturity. This can happen because of various dangerous reasons.

My cry to any true follower of Jesus is to be humble, acquainted with the scriptures, open to rebuke, accessible to wise spiritual counsel and led by the Holy Spirit enough to always be willing to receive conviction whenever it comes knocking at the door. It is a serious matter to find yourself not being convicted at the times you should be. This means that you are rejecting, ignoring or smothering the Holy Spirit in some way. It is because of the work of the Holy Spirit that a person is granted opportunities to be convicted and to properly receive rebuke and correction. Indeed it is a tremendous grace gift to have opportunities of conviction because each time it brings you to a fork in the road where you can choose to be a bit more like Jesus or continue to be much more like yourself.

Please understand that He brings conviction through the scriptures, circumstances and other people. Yes, these other people are flawed as well. It is important in this day an age to remember that having flaws does not take away anyone's ability to be used as a tool by which the Holy Spirit can bring conviction and correction to you. Just understand the importance of receiving it whenever it comes. You do not want to get to a place where you are of a reprobate state of mind or your conscience has been seared.

All in all, it is good to understand that condemning people is not a good thing. We were never charged to condemn anyone. Though this is true, condemning the actions of people is completely different and can help. Informing people that their condemning actions could possibly condemn them in the future is quite beneficial for them. Any Bible reader should understand this concept through the many examples of the apostles, prophets and even Jesus executing this within the Bible. It is good to know the difference between what should and should not be done when it comes to condemnation. Think about the many different types of condemning statements that friends and family members make from time to time: "You are never going to amount to anything." "You will be just like your father when you grow up (in a bad way)." "You can't do anything right." These are condemning statements that we should avoid, not statements backed by the Bible that may make people feel bad or convicted at times. As long as we bring proper conviction with their best interest in mind and without pride in our hearts, at times, this will do more good than harm regardless of the person feeling bad as a result of what is said.

A good key that sums it up is this: Remember, we are not here to destroy people. We are here to help them not be destroyed.

"HOMOSEXUALITY IS PEOPLE"

Given the title of this chapter, it is important to understand that this is not an attempt to say that those who struggle with or embrace any parts of homosexuality are not humans. This is in no way, an attempt to say that those diving into this lifestyle are any less than humans. This is absolutely not the notion here. The reason for exposing this Goliath portion of The New Age Vernacular is to show plainly how this agenda was tailor-made to bait the masses. This agenda baits those in the lifestyle as well as those that will never consider partaking in homosexual activity. It baits those outside the church as well as inside the church. As a matter of fact, this portion of The New Age Vernacular is largely responsible for the present largest split between "church people". It is the reason why the world presently attempts to accommodate homosexuality in legislation. Why do I say "tailor-made"? It is vitally important to understand that the homosexual movement would have never taken off without having done two things first: 1. Reverse a mental illness (call the sick well and the well sick). 2. Make a sin into person. These two things contribute significantly to the current impact of this movement.

1. *The reversing of a mental illness*

To get the masses to accept and embrace homosexuality, the historic negative stigma attached to homosexuality had to be erased, after which the process of normalizing the behavior could begin. To assist in getting society to cease seeing this in a negative way, they had to stop getting society to see it as an illness. With mental illness attached to homosexuality, it emphasized the problematic aspects of it, not just to the church but even throughout the secular world. In 1973 the American Psychiatric Association removed the diagnosis of homosexuality from the second edition of the DSM (Diagnostic and Statistical Manual), which helped normalize homosexuality but it did not stop there.

Constructing the term "homophobia" catapulted this concept to an entirely different level which brought society to the point of no return. This not only cleared those bound by homosexuality but also made the lens even cloudier by attaching a label of illness to anyone that still viewed homosexuality as an illness or did not agree with the lifestyle. This was so very strategic because it attached a mental illness to true Christians and anyone else that doesn't agree with and support homosexuality.

When people are labeled in a negative way by society, it motivates them to prove that they are not what that label implies.

As a result, many now have a reason to escape or avoid the negative label of "homophobia" and the ridicule that comes with it. How does one escape being labeled as "homophobic"? Simply by being seen agreeing with, promoting, embracing and/or defending homosexuality as well as those bound by it's grips. Unfortunately, now people would rather mishandle this subject by overcorrecting to seemingly prove their love and support for the LGBT group instead being labeled "homophobic".

2. Making the sin a person

The main thrust that enabled this movement to take off and penetrate almost every area in society was when this particular sin was made into people. When homosexuality started being accepted and treated as an inherent trait, things began to get tricky.

Why is it that people mostly view all the other sins in a way that is easier to make a distinction between the act or actions and the people committing the acts except for homosexuality? Why is it that even the unsaved world, at least presently, can maintain the difference between the people that commit physical abuse and the physical abuse itself? Why is it that when it comes to rapists, molesters, wife beaters, drug abusers and alcoholics the world can separate the people from their bad behaviors or addictions? Why is it that the world and now even many "church people" do not make that separation when it comes to the LGBT community? Why is it that most would find it absurd to allow an alcoholic during the time of their drunken stupor, an adulterer while committing adultery, a man beating his wife, and a drug user while abusing drugs to dwell in a church service but see no problem with allowing cross-dressers and "transgender" people to have that right?

Would the church be split on the issue of the homosexual lifestyle if society had never made this particular sin a person? Once this sin started to be viewed as people, all the sympathy, rights, love and compassion that people should have, this sin now has.

In some of my previous teachings, I have mentioned that we are living in a time where the increase of wickedness is riding on the bed of undisciplined hearts. If Satan is good at anything, it is playing the role of the victim. Perceived victimization, increased wickedness and undisciplined hearts are the recipe for the sympathy for evil. When it comes to homosexuality, sympathy for evil has become more widespread and partly because this sin is now seen as a certain type of person.

The Bible makes a distinction between the sin and the people who embrace it. The scriptures do not recognize, what many would call "the homosexual community", as some different type of created beings that were born a certain way. The word of God notes homosexuality not as people but a sin that people commit. Let's take a look at some verses. **Romans 1:26-27 (KJV) reads: "26. For this cause God gave them up unto vile affections: for even their women did change the natural use into that which is against nature: 27. And likewise also the men, leaving the natural use of the woman, burned in their lust one toward another; men with men working that which is unseemly, and receiving in themselves that recompence of their error which was meet."** Notice the line ". . . *burned in their lust one toward another.*" This verse notes homosexuality as something that the men and women began to do because of their lust.

1 Timothy 1:10 (KJV) reads: **"For whoremongers, for them that defile themselves with mankind, for men stealers, for liars, for perjured persons, and if there be any other thing that is contrary to sound doctrine."** Here again the scriptures note it as something that the people *did* and not something they *were*. Here is the same verse in another translation. **1 Timothy 1:10 (ESV): "the sexually immoral, men who practice homosexuality."** In addition, **1 Corinthians 6:9-10 (KJV) reads: "Know ye not that the unrighteous shall not inherit the kingdom of God? Be not deceived: neither fornicators, nor**

112

idolaters, nor effeminate, nor abusers of themselves with mankind, 10. Nor thieves, nor covetous, nor drunkards, nor revilers, nor extortioners, shall inherit the kingdom of God." Here it notes it as "abusers of themselves with mankind". This describes people that abused themselves and not people who were simply being themselves. Here is the same verse in another translation. **1 Corinthians 6:9 (AMP): "Do you not know that the unrighteous will not inherit or have any share in the kingdom of God? Do not be deceived; neither the sexually immoral, nor idolaters, nor effeminate [by perversion], nor those who participate in homosexuality."** Once again we see homosexuality noted as something that some participate in and not some different type of race of people.

In some translations, it may seem as though the scriptures describe homosexuality as a people because of the term "homosexuals". **1 Timothy 1:10 (AMP)** reads: **"for sexually immoral persons, for homosexuals, for kidnappers and slave traders, for liars, for perjurers-and for whatever else is contrary to sound doctrine."** **1 Corinthians 6:9 (NAS): "Or do you not know that the unrighteous will not inherit the kingdom of God? Do not be deceived; neither fornicators, nor idolaters, nor adulterers, nor effeminate, nor homosexuals."** There is really no need to be alarmed here because even with these differences, the meaning of these verses do not change.

An example to help further this point is that of "a speeder" and a person that drives over the speed limit. When law enforcement says something like "we are cracking down on speeders in this area," they are simply speaking about people that are committing a crime by driving too many miles over the speed limit. They are not speaking of a different type of group of people who were speeders from birth. Are speeders people? Yes! Are they a different type of people? No! They are simply people that are attached to certain unsafe actions. Do they need more rights as speeders? Absolutely not. The reason why speeders do not need more "rights" is because they already have rights as people. Though they have rights as people, their behaviors do not have rights. My brothers and sisters of the faith, this is where a major line of distinction should have been made; because it has not, however, deceit surrounds the entire movement of those in the homosexual community as well as any that support and stand in defense of the community. When it comes to rights, it is not a matter of them fighting for their rights as people; they are fighting for the rights of their behaviors and way of thinking. Simply put, the LGBT community and their supporters are not fighting for rights as people; they are fighting for the rights of their sins.

Whenever a society advocates for, preserves, justifies and defends sin, that same society is fighting in support of its own deterioration.

In many ways it would have been helpful if we would have started with addressing the behaviors instead of starting with the people that love the behaviors. If we would start with the behaviors and the negative spiritual and physical impact they have on those participating and those around them, out of genuine concern and care for these individuals, we could see that certain behaviors are bad for them regardless of their attraction and addiction to them. This is one reason why it is easily seen and understood by most that there should be no fighting for "speeders' rights". By looking at the actions of speeding first, it is determined that speeding itself is bad for speeders regardless of how much they love it, embrace it, are addicted to it, and do not feel as if they can change their feelings toward speeding. Whether the world will ever be able to see this or not, those who are a part of the true remnant of God should be able to and respond accordingly.

Again, out of genuine concern for their well-being as well as those surrounding them, it is best that restrictions and boundaries remain in place. It is the same for those that are addicted to drugs. It is easily understood that we cannot just go and fight for the rights of drug addicts to be strung out just because they love what they do and cannot seem to fight the urges that keep them attached and addicted. Why can't it be just as easily seen when it comes to homosexuality and the like? The answer to this question is quite simple. It is because television, radio and the internet has manipulated the minds of the masses. Some may say "well that is different", when it comes to homosexuality and everything else. If it is different, why can't this difference be seen within any content of scripture? Again, it is only seen as different by most because the media has consistently told them to see it differently. It's important to realize that a lie often repeated, becomes true to the one that often hears and receives it.

One reason this has been submitted to the masses is to motivate society to now see and treat the sin of homosexuality as people who are now being born that way. There are many inside and outside of the church that are on both sides of this argument. While there is no such thing as a gay gene, spirits and generational habits can attach themselves to a certain kindred. There is normally dangerous thinking that hangs around the notion that a person can be born gay because it's attached to the fact that this person can't help how they were born and therefore it is assumed that nothing can be done about it. If nothing can be done about it, the only thing left to do is to accept it.

These facts are irrelevant to handling this subject matter regardless if you feel people can be born homosexual or not. **Psalms 51:5 (KJV) Behold I was shapen in iniquity; and in sin did my mother conceive me. Ephesians 2:1-3 (ESV) And you were dead in the trespasses and sins ²in which you once walked, following the course of this world, following the prince of the power of the air, the spirit that is now at work in the sons of disobedience— ³among whom we all once lived in the passions of our flesh, carrying out the desires of the body[a] and the mind, and were by nature children of wrath, like the rest of mankind.**

Given these passages of scripture, it is important to realize that 100% of mankind was born as sinners needing a savior. It is because of the grace and mercy of God through the blood sacrifice of Jesus Christ that any who is willing can be regenerated and changed from the life and identity of sin into a new creation! No matter how much sin is embraced and endorsed by the world, it is crucial to never forget that the blood still works. It is still changing lives and setting the captives free from all matter of bondages. So whether a person was born that way or became that way, it doesn't change the fact that God is not pleased with a homosexual condition just like He is not pleased with any other sinful condition. The good thing is that something can still be done about it.

"UNITY"

Every time we hear words like unity, unifying, coming together, working together, and being in harmony, it is important to understand that they are not necessarily godly things. Is God a God of unity? Yes, He is. Just as it is important to know that God loves unity, it is as equally important to understand that God is not the only one. Satan the adversary has a plan for unity as well. Throughout scripture, even starting as early as Genesis, Satan had a way of counterfeiting or providing alternatives to godly things and concepts. Look at what he proposed to Eve. Look at the fact that he went to Eve so that she could be "enlightened" first. Though theirs were swallowed up, the magicians of Egypt were able to make serpents out of their staffs just as Moses and Aaron did. 2 Corinthians lets us know that just as Satan appears as an angel of light, his workers go around masquerading as apostles of Christ. Given all of this, it would not be a foreign thing for Satan to have a counterfeit form of unity.

Kingdom citizens must understand that just because God wants unity, He is not going to settle for just any form of it. Please know that God does NOT want the world to be unified. He does not want all religions to be unified. God ONLY wants unity in the midst of His people that are a part of His spiritual family. His ultimate desire is not that different faiths and various types of people come together for good causes. Often times we as Christians seem to forget that God's main concern is for the safety and preservation of the bride of Christ and He would not be in favor of anything that would come against that. This is one of the reasons why Paul instructed not to be found eating with a certain type of person. Satan's ambition for his unity is to merge with, to corrupt, to blur the lines, and to taint a pure thing. Satan has always wanted to taint the church by merging with the church.

This is why it is not a good idea or good strategy for Christian celebrities and artists to join forces with workers of the kingdom of darkness for the sake of "reaching" more people of Christ. This is why it is not ideal for Christian leaders to be so inviting of worldly people into their churches to assist them in "ministry". When people defend things like this, they do it in the name of "reaching" people as if Satan has no arms himself.

Let's review some scriptures for the Biblical take on unity. **Psalm 133:1 (KJV) reads: "Behold, how good and how pleasant it is for brethren to dwell together in unity."** Note here that the word "brethren" indicates those of the same family.

Ephesians 4:11-13 (KJV): "And he gave some, apostles, and some, prophets; and some, evangelists; and some, pastors and teachers; 12. For the perfecting of the saints, for the work of

the ministry, for the edifying of the body of Christ: **13. Till we all come in the unity of the faith, and of the knowledge of the Son of God, unto a perfect man, unto the measure of the stature of the fullness of Christ."** Verse 13 clearly refers to the unity of the faith. The context of this passage of scripture does not speak to the world but to the perfecting of the saints. The ministry gifts mentioned in verse 11 were for the benefit of Christians and those who would become Christians in the future. Therefore, the unity spoken of here is for the family of God. In moving up to the beginning of this same chapter, we have **Ephesians 4:3 (KJV): "Endeavouring to keep the unity of the spirit in the bond of peace."** This speaks of the unity of the spirit for the body of Christ. This can be better understood when glancing at the following verse 4, which speaks of there being one body and one spirit. This same verse in the Amplified Version reads, **"There is one body [of believers] and one Spirit . . ."**

I want to end this book with a plea to the church at large. This plea comes by way of the last scripture that will be used in dealing with godly unity. **1 Corinthians 1:10 (KJV) reads: "Now I beseech you, brethren, by the name of our Lord Jesus Christ, that ye all speak the same thing, and that there be no divisions among you; but that ye be perfectly joined together in the same mind and in the same judgement."** Get this verse in your heart and mind. Let's review the Amplified Version: **1 Corinthians 1:10 (AMP): "But I urge you, believers, by the name of our Lord Jesus Christ, that all of you be in full agreement in what you say, and that there be no divisions or factions among you, but that you be perfectly united in your way of thinking and in your judgement [about the matters of the faith]."** Pay attention to what is being said here when it mentions **"in full agreement"**, **"united in your way of thinking and in your judgement."**

I do understand that we are living in a world where there are now more denominations than pages in the Bible. Additionally, we are living in a day where there is a growing pride behind the right, ability and freedom to disagree. Sadly this has grown quite significantly among professing believers. Remember, having a right to do something does not always make it right. Humility is what it is because it does not exercise all of its rights because humility understands its right to relinquish rights. I am not saying that we all will agree on everything all of the time but we should agree on many more things than we do and not be so "all over the place". I know it seems far away and impossible but none of these facts are reason enough to not strive in the brotherly spirit that can bring this to pass.

Take a moment and honestly ask yourself this question: When it comes to the Body of Christ, do I strive to say the same thing or my own thing? If you were to say the right answer to this question and truly mean it, what should accompany this is a humility that would allow your beliefs about certain topics and portions of the Bible and ways of thinking to be measured and corrected by the Holy Scriptures and godly wise council. We have to renew our minds to the point that we will not stay married to certain thoughts and beliefs just because they are what we believed first and what we have been believing the longest. Be free from the power of THE FIRST LIE! Have the humility to allow all of your thoughts and beliefs to be examined by scripture along with the assistance of those that have studied the Bible with a disciplined heart (and yes they will be another flawed human being). In times of disagreement with fellow believers (on things that can be conclusive), we should all be willing to say, "Either you are wrong,

I am wrong or we are both wrong, but if you show me the error in my way, I'm willing to change and advocate whatever the truth is regardless of how long I've believed whatever I've believed and regardless of what and who it may cost me." Let's allow the Holy Spirit to discipline our hearts to where the content of the scriptures become our filter of life!

Please be diligent in sharing this information of The New Age Vernacular. It indeed is one of the timeliest and most relevant topics given the times in which we live. This truly can assist in guarding the foundational message of the Gospel of Jesus Christ. This can assist in strengthening the true remnant of the Kingdom of God today. It could literally mean spiritual life or death for some people. Understanding The New Age Vernacular will help Christians not to voluntarily silence their voices which, in turn, will bring life that frees people from the grips of spiritual ignorance and blindness. This is a tool that can strategically encourage the saints to bring true Godly love to a rapidly declining society and dying world. No more shall we allow the world to reach and penetrate the borders of the true church with this new age language. No more shall we allow this language to corner the world view and the presentation of the gospel! No more shall we be bound by The

New Age Vernacular! Deliverance has come and a portion of ignorance is receding! Let's do what we can to expose this prevalent but subtle tool. Remember that the kingdom of darkness is preserved and allowed to roam as it wills with the silencing of God's people!

I must leave you with this reminder. Most people will not welcome the exposure of The New Age Vernacular. We are not here to make the world upset but the world will be upset simply because of our nature in Christ. Jesus did not aim to make people upset but He was willing to do things that made people upset for the sake of the Kingdom and even for the betterment of those that became upset. Prevalence should never determine whether something is now acceptable. Never determine if something you are bringing to others is good or right based on how it is accepted or rejected by man. Keep in mind that Jesus not only brought good things but also was the good thing. Despite this fact, look at how many times men rejected Him and His ways even to the point of them wanting Him tortured and dead.

This is one reason why every true follower of Christ needs consistent fellowship with like-minded believers. This helps reinforce your Kingdom mindset regardless of the blind's rejection. True saints need to be encouraged to be steadfast, unmovable and not weary in doing well. Keep in mind that we do not fit. We are in this world but not of it. Yes, they are going to call you a bunch of things but they called Jesus worse. Yes, family, co-workers and some self-proclaiming Christians will not understand because you are speaking a foreign language. Sometimes you will need to encourage yourself by looking at what people called the biblical prophets, Paul and Jesus. If you are being called similar things, then you may be doing something right. Did He not tell us that the world would hate us because of who we are in Him?

I will close with the following verses: **John 15:18-25 (KJV): "If the world hate you, ye know that it hated me before it hated you. 19. If ye were of the world, the world would love his own: but because ye are not of the world, but I have chosen you out of the world, therefore the world hateth you. 20. Remember the word that I said unto you, The servant is not greater than his lord. If they have persecuted me, they will also persecute you; if they have kept my saying, they will keep yours also. 21. But all these things will they do unto you for my name's sake, because they know not him that sent me. 22. If I had not come and spoken unto them, they had not sin: but now they have no cloke for their sin. 23. He that hateth me hateth my Father also. 24. If I had not done among them the works which none other man did, they had not had sin: but now have they both seen and hated both me and my Father. 25. But this**

cometh to pass, that the word might be fulfilled that is written in their law, They hated me without a cause." Remember you are on the winning side even if it does not feel like it at times. REMAIN STRONG AND STEADFAST IN BEING A PART OF THE TRUE REMNANT! Please be diligent in sharing this information of The New Age Vernacular.

*"To escape the grips of this world, one must have the **DISCERNMENT** to notice repetitious cycles, the **WILL** to break those cycles and the **FORTITUDE** to continuously go against the grain of what those cycles and the world deems as normal."*

-Andrew Crawley jr

VISIT OUR WEBSITE:

AndrewCrawleyJr.com

for more information and products!

For booking email:
Andrew@AndrewCrawleyJr.com